T0281775

BREAKING THE CODE

Otto Preminger

versus

Hollywood's Censors

Plus

CODE BLUE!

A Play by
Arnie Reisman & Nat Segaloff

APPLAUSE
THEATRE & CINEMA BOOKS
ESSEX, CONNECTICUT

APPLAUSE
THEATRE & CINEMA BOOKS

An imprint of Globe Pequot, the trade division of The Rowman & Littlefield Publishing Group, Inc.
4501 Forbes Blvd., Ste. 200
Lanham, MD 20706
www.rowman.com

Distributed by NATIONAL BOOK NETWORK

Breaking the Code: Otto Preminger versus Hollywood's Censors
Text © 2022 by Nat Segaloff. Play ©2004 by Arnie Reisman & Nat Segaloff

Library of Congress Cataloging-in-Publication Data available

Names: Segaloff, Nat, author. | Segaloff, Nat. Code blue.
Title: Breaking the code : Otto Preminger versus Hollywood's censors / by Nat Segaloff. "Code blue" / a play by Arnie Resiman & Nat Segaloff.
Description: Essex, Connecticut : Applause, [2023] | Includes bibliographical references and index.
Identifiers: LCCN 2022056711 (print) | LCCN 2022056712 (ebook) | ISBN 9781493074884 (cloth) | ISBN 9781493074891 (ebook)
Subjects: LCSH: Preminger, Otto. | Motion picture producers and directors—United States—Biography. | Motion pictures—Censorship—United States—History. | Breen, Joseph Ignatius, 1890-1965. | Motion pictures—United States—History—20th century. | Moon is blue (Motion picture) —Drama. | Preminger, Otto—Drama. | Breen, Joseph Ignatius, 1890-1965—Drama. | Motion pictures—Censorship—United States—History—Drama.
Classification: LCC PN1998.3.P743 S44 2023 (print) | LCC PN1998.3.P743 (ebook) | DDC 791.4302/33092 [B] —dc23/eng/20230203
LC record available at https://lccn.loc.gov/2022056711
LC ebook record available at https://lccn.loc.gov/2022056712

™ The paper used in this publication meets the minimum requirements of American National Standard for Information Sciences—Permanence of Paper for Printed Library Materials, ANSI/NISO Z39.48-1992

WARNING

This book contains correspondence between the Production Code Administration and the filmmaking community that includes language and descriptions of actions that some people may find offensive. These are offered for scholarly and historical purposes. If you are more offended by language than the idea of censoring it, you probably shouldn't be reading this—or voting, leaving the house, or procreating.

For Arnie Reisman,
Collaborator, Mentor, Friend

Contents

CONTENTS

Introduction and Acknowledgments

This is not a history of the Production Code. There are already enough of those ranging from more or less official (*The Hays Code* by Raymond Moley [New York: Bobbs-Merrill, 1945]) to personal (*See No Evil* by Jack Vizzard [New York: Simon & Schuster, 1970]) to wry (*The Censorship Papers* by Gerald Gardner [New York: Dodd, Mead & Company, 1987]) to scholarly (*Hollywood v. Hard Core: How the Struggle over Censorship Saved the Modern Film Industry* by Jon Lewis [New York: New York University Press, 2000]). All of them, plus the endless other books, academic papers, and memoirs, describe a system of self-censorship that shaped not only the movies turned out by the studios during the four decades it was in force but also its intransigence against the maturing sensibilities of American moviegoers.

Rather, this book is about the efforts of one man, director-producer Otto Preminger, to bring his aesthetic vision to the screen even if it meant challenging the Production Code. Along the way, he sent shock waves not only through Hollywood but also through a network of exhibitors, publishers, and religious leaders who had a personal, even financial, stake in the repression of artistic freedom.

Telling this story was a matter of connecting certain dots. The process began in 2003 when Arnie Reisman and I thought it might be interesting to write a play about Preminger's efforts to get a Code seal for his 1954 romantic comedy *The Moon Is Blue*, based on F. Hugh Herbert's 1951 play. In those days, no film could be shown that did not receive authorization from Hollywood's self-censoring agency, the Production Code Administration, and *The Moon Is Blue* was deemed too "adult" even for adults to see. In our analysis, the obstacle was not only the calcified restrictions of the Code itself but also the almost personal opposition from its administrator, Joseph I. Breen. Even though *Moon* had run on Broadway without reaction from the censors, Breen was prepared to go to war to save the rest of the country from its sensibilities. (A synopsis will follow.)

Breen was not the stereotypical pinch-faced, sourpuss, bluenosed censor. He was an articulate, intelligent, worldly, and diplomatic man who was tasked with saying "no" to filmmakers and studio moguls earning many times his salary and controlling the careers of thousands of people.

Preminger was no slouch, either. Educated in Germany as a trial lawyer before switching to theatre under the influential Max Reinhardt, he was an urbane and savvy opponent and clever political operative. Arnie and I decided to make our play, which we titled *Code Blue!*, into a clash between these two evenly matched but wildly disparate titans. Naturally, it had to be a comedy.

Once written, however, no one wanted to produce it. Nobody we showed it to was scared; worse, we couldn't even get anybody to read it. All people said, in various ways, was that they didn't think artistic freedom was commercial (even though they benefited from it every time they raised their curtains). So we escorted our manuscript to a nice comfortable folder on our respective external hard drives, where it had lots of company with other projects that never got past the ones-and-zeros stage.

Then Arnie died on October 4, 2021. It was a blow to decades of our friendship and all the projects we could have done together in the future. It was then that I took our play off the digital shelf and reread it to relive the fun we'd had writing it. Then the memory of another friend swam to mind.

In 1975, I was hired by Twentieth Century-Fox to dole out something called cooperative advertising. This involved allotting money to theatres to run ads for the Fox films they were showing. I worked out of a small office in the Burlington Building on Sixth Avenue in New York City. To say that the job was stultifying is to be kind. My boss, however, was a true old-world gentleman. He was Nico Jacobellis, whom I had known for several years as a fellow publicist before I was brought under his direct supervision. Unlike I, who chafed at toting up dollars and newspaper lineage, Nico accepted, even relished, the boredom. It was as though he were trying to bury some unwanted excitement in his past. I knew what it was, but each time I tried to bring it up, he brushed the subject aside. You see, Nico was part of Hollywood history. In 1964, he had been the manager at the Cleveland, Ohio, theatre that was showing Louis Malle's *The Lovers* when cops busted the place for showing an obscene film. As the named defendant in the landmark *Jacobellis v. Ohio*, 378 U.S. 187 (1964), Nico was eventually absolved when the U.S. Supreme Court overturned his conviction. Justice William Brennan wrote for the SCOTUS majority that films should be judged by national standards, not local community standards, and that, by that measure, *The Lovers* was not obscene. In 1952, it was followed by *Burstyn v. Wilson*, 343 U.S. 495 (1952), over the film *The Miracle*, which, at last, accorded First Amendment protection to motion pictures as a form of artistic expression.[1]

Burstyn was a victory for freedom of speech and began pressure to liberalize, if not abolish, the Production Code. That would take another sixteen years.

Not every conflict with screen freedom wound up in court. Indeed, that's what the Production Code was established to prevent; rather than tarnish Hollywood's tinsel with an obscenity trial, the industry labored to head off scandal at the earliest stage: before a film was made. And this is where the battle begins between filmmaker Otto Preminger and the Code.

In the twenty-two years between 1944 and 1966, Preminger clashed, first with Joseph Breen and then with his successor, Geoffrey Shurlock, over nine films with which he was involved: *Laura*, *Forever Amber*, *The Moon Is Blue*, *Carmen Jones*, *The Man with the Golden Arm*, *Saint Joan*, *Anatomy of a Murder*, *Advise & Consent*, and *Hurry Sundown*. The first two were the responsibility of his studio, Twentieth Century-Fox, where he was a hired director. When he became his own producer, however, he had to fight his own fights, and he did not shy away from any of them despite the often-unknowable workings of the Production Code. The details of each skirmish vary, but they cover the same landscape: art versus commerce, freedom of speech versus censorship, and money versus principle.

Times may have changed, but those battles continue, especially as "cancel culture" imposes itself on discourse in American society. This book is an attempt to go back and see how walls can be made to crumble.

This book could not exist in its present form without the extraordinary support of the staff of the Margaret Herrick Library of the Academy Foundation of the Academy of Motion Picture Arts and Sciences, which houses the internal files of the Production Code Administration. In that regard, Elizabeth Youle and Genevieve Maxwell of the National Film Information Service have my undying gratitude for their encouragement and assistance. I also appreciate the American Civil Liberties Union of Southern California (Hector Villagra, executive director) and the Massachusetts Civil Liberties Union (Carol Rose, executive director), my literary agent Lee Sobel, and Pamela Chais and Diana Markes, the daughters of playwright F. Hugh Herbert, for their early enthusiasm and guidance when *Code Blue!* was first being written.

It is hard to express my thanks, or my grief, for my friend and writing partner Arnie Reisman. A man of many talents (writer, editor, producer, poet, performer, husband, wit, etc.), he seemed immortal. Now only his memory is. I was privileged to be his friend for half a century, and I grieve not only for his wife, Paula Lyons, but also for those who will never have the joy of knowing him.

Special thanks to Applause Theatre & Cinema Books for their dedication to the history of our craft, particularly John Cerullo, Chris Chappell, Barbara Claire, Jessica Kastner, Laurel Myers and Della Vache for a productive collaboration.

Finally, I thank filmmakers whom I have known over the years who benefited from the Code's demise and counseled me on their craft. They are, alphabetically, Robert Altman, James Bridges, William Friedkin, Larry Gelbart, William Gibson, Sir Christopher Hampton, Arthur Penn, Michael Ritchie, Martin Ritt, Mark Rydell, and Peter Yates. Finally, I thank Otto Preminger (sorry about last billing, Otto), whom I met socially several times and for whom I handled publicity during his later career with his long-suffering executive assistant Nat Rudich. All of these artists spoke about the twinge you get in your stomach when you're about to do something that you think might start a backlash. In their cases, they ignored it, but for a world that is now awash in cancel culture, the threat is worse, for it comes not from external forces of repression but from within.

—Nat Segaloff, Los Angeles

1

THE CODE

Some say it was all Fatty Arbuckle's fault. Others blame Mabel Normand. Still others cite William Desmond Taylor, Mary Miles Minter, Thomas Ince, or Wallace Reid. While the rest of America was roaring in that fabled decade of the Twenties, Hollywood was screaming with scandals, all of them datelined Tinseltown.

Admittedly, the film community was asking for it. The movies as a commercial enterprise had begun barely twenty years earlier by appealing to immigrant, working-class, and largely illiterate audiences. The carriage trade would have nothing to do with the first Nickelodeons and, not trusting the market to level itself, leveraged their moral snobbery on the flickers. It was hard to find a city or community without a self-nominated standards league bent on protecting the lower classes while, in actuality, conspiring with the authorities to keep the unwashed in their place. At first, there were cries for government censorship of the "flickers" in the form of licensing Nickelodeon parlors and "long-store" exhibition halls (converted funeral parlors made excellent auditoriums), dictating what they could show. Exhibitors were mindful of public pressure and succumbed to it the way sideshow barkers might tone down their pitches when the local cop saunters by. One of the most famous examples of this compliance is Thomas Edison's censoring of a film clip of Fatima, the exotic dancing hit of the 1896 Chicago Exposition. Although she was fully clothed, in fact overly clothed, censors insisted on obscuring the jiggly bits with superimposed white fences. Somehow Eugene Sandow, the nearly nude German muscleman, got away unfenced. As frivolous as these compromises may seem today, they were the first act in a movement to control screen content.

But first it's important to understand the gap between what comes under the protection of the First Amendment to the United States Constitution and what does not.

Although the First Amendment specifies that "Congress shall make no law . . . abridging the freedom of speech, or of the press," the trick in the text is that, while Congress—meaning the government—shall make no law, etc., other entities can and often do. Civil libertarians note that the word *censorship* properly applies only to the government. Organizations such as internet sites, periodicals, communications companies, and private schools may censor whatever they wish as long as they receive no government funding. According to the American Civil Liberties Union, "Censorship by the government is unconstitutional. In contrast, when private individuals or groups organize boycotts against stores that sell magazines of which they disapprove, their actions are protected by the First Amendment, although they can become dangerous in the extreme. Private pressure groups, not the government, promulgated and enforced the infamous Hollywood blacklists during the McCarthy period. But these private censorship campaigns are best countered by groups and individuals speaking out and organizing in defense of the threatened expression."[1]

The distinction between government and private censorship is crucial, and forces of repression have embraced, ignored, and misunderstood it for a century. If one's private employer forbids certain language or ideas, it's permitted but not if the government does it.[2] But not always; surprisingly, it was not until 1918 that the First Amendment, which was passed in 1791, was tested in court, and it lost. On June 16, 1918, prominent Socialist labor leader and political candidate Eugene V. Debs spoke outside the Canton, Ohio, prison. He told his audience of over a thousand people that he supported three incarcerated Socialists who had been convicted of violating the Sedition Act. He condemned the then ongoing Great War (he was a pacifist) and even told the crowd that he had to mind his words because of potential repercussion. His caution bore out; he was arrested and convicted of obstructing military recruitment and enlistment. Handed a ten-year sentence, he appealed his conviction with the argument that his measured words did not violate the First Amendment. Debs suffered from bad timing. Just one week before the U.S. Supreme Court decided *Debs v. United States*, 249 U.S. 211 (1919), Supreme Court Justice Oliver Wendell Holmes—often thought of as a liberal—had written of a "clear and present danger" in his opinion in *Schenck v. United States* (1919), saying that judges must consider the context of a speech as well as its specific words. President Warren G. Harding commuted Debs's sentence in 1921, the same year that Roger Baldwin, Crystal Eastman, Jane Addams, Norman Thomas, and Felix Frankfurter formed what became the American Civil Liberties Union (ACLU), whose primary mission is defending the First Amendment.[3] Since that time, numerous First Amendment cases—many brought by the ACLU—have been adjudicated before the U.S. Supreme Court, which, despite leaning to the right on many issues, tends to support freedom of speech (at least as of this writing).

* * *

Nevertheless, the U.S. Supreme Court opened the door to government censorship in 1915 when it decided, in *Mutual Film Corp. v. Industrial Commission of Ohio*, 236 U.S. 230 (1915), that motion pictures were a commercial endeavor and, as such, did not deserve First Amendment protection.[4] While the Court would reverse its own decision in 1952 with *The Miracle* case (*Burstyn v. Wilson*, q.v.), the intervening years saw ongoing tension between screen speech and screen freedom, and local censorship boards took note. But the heavy move toward censorship began not when the industry was just getting started in the East but with the rise of the studio system in the 1920s in Southern California. The emergence of large production, distribution, and exhibition concerns such as Universal (1912), Paramount (1914), Warner Bros. (1923), Columbia (1924), MGM (1924), and RKO (1928) began the consolidation of commercial filmmaking. As public corporations beholden to stockholders, they were particularly vulnerable to intimidation from pressure groups. Moreover, as corporations founded and run exclusively by Jews in an era when America was tolerating the Ku Klux Klan and deporting Reds, the founding moguls were keenly aware of the need to maintain a low profile and high moral standards. It is against this background that the spotlight was thrown on Hollywood.

It has been said that when you take the most attractive and talented people in the world and put them all in one city, sparks are bound to fly. And fly they did:[5]

4

- March 28, 1920: Mary Pickford marries Douglas Fairbanks, consolidating their status as the Queen and King of Hollywood. What tarnishes their union is that they had been having an affair while still married to other people, and even though they get divorced so they can marry each other, the moguls are concerned that America will not accept divorced celebrities. (They do.)

- September 10, 1920. Young actress Olive Thomas (Oliva R. Duffy) dies in Paris five days after drinking mercury dichloride, a syphilis medication meant for her husband, Jack Pickford, the young brother of America's Sweetheart Mary Pickford. Both Thomas and husband Pickford are stars for the Lewis J. Selznick studios, which hangs on for dear life while the story develops. Apparently, Olive had gone to Paris ahead of Jack and, rather than visit the fancy fashion salons as her publicist said, was burning her candle at both ends in the City of Lights. Her suicide, it began to be rumored, was because she was unable to buy heroin to give her addicted husband when he arrived. Little Mary survived this double scandal as she did her divorce.

- September 3, 1921. Beloved Paramount Pictures comedian Roscoe "Fatty" Arbuckle drives to San Francisco's St. Francis Hotel for a Labor Day weekend of either relaxation or drinking (depending which press account is to be believed), having just wrapped a tiring six feature films in a row down in Hollywood. Two friends travel with him: Fred Fishback and Lowell Sherman. Despite Prohibition, the bootleg liquor flows. People start joining Arbuckle in suite 1221, including a young actress named Virginia Rappé, her friend Maude Delmont, and any number of hangers-on.[6] Shortly, Rappé becomes sick from the alcohol and is put chastely to bed by Arbuckle, who must leave for an appointment. The hotel doctor and nurse confirm that, other than intoxication, Rappé appears uninjured. Three days later, however, Rappé is taken to the hospital, where, on September 10, she dies. An examination of her medical records reveals that one of her internal organs had ruptured and nobody in the hospital had noticed. Moreover, those at the hospital who performed the autopsy remove and dispose of her internal organs. It was subsequently established that she died of complications of an illegal abortion. Now the spinning begins courtesy of Maude Delmont, who, according to researcher David Yallop, was a well-known extortionist, bigamist, and all-around reprobate. It was she who tells headline-hungry Hearst newspapers that Arbuckle killed Rappé during intercourse by laying on top of her. Delmont is considered such an unreliable witness that she is never called to the stand, but her story spreads in the headlines. District Attorney Matthew Brady, eager to run for governor, pushes for a charge of murder, but the judge lowers it to manslaughter. Arbuckle endures three trials: two ending with hung juries and the third with exoneration after Rappé's medical history is revealed. Not only does the jury return a verdict of not guilty, they issue a public apology to Arbuckle. Nevertheless, Paramount boss Adolph Zukor, fearful of public reaction, cancels Arbuckle's contract, pulls his films from release, and makes this once-popular comedian a virtual nonperson.

- February 1, 1922. Director William Desmond Taylor is murdered in his Hollywood home. A neighbor, Charles Chaplin's former leading lady, Edna Purviance, calls comedienne Mabel Normand, who calls Paramount (still reeling from the Arbuckle scandal), where she is under contract. Purviance then calls actress Mary Miles

Minter's mother, Charlotte Selby. Mabel speeds to Taylor's house to fetch her love letters while Selby hurries to be with her daughter. At some point, somebody finally thinks of calling the police. Subsequent press reports uncover that Mary Miles Minter was also involved with Taylor and that both she and Normand had called on the doomed director on the night of his death. Eventually, the news breaks that not only was Taylor involved with Minter and Normand but also seeing Selby. The murder lay unsolved for years until writer Sidney D. Kirkpatrick published *A Cast of Killers* (1986), which uncovers that director King Vidor had followed a trail of clues to deduce that it was Charlotte Selby who shot Taylor for two-timing her with her daughter. (Vidor's and Kirkpatrick's conclusion is disputed.) After the book is published, the film rights are purchased by none other than Paramount Pictures, which, for some reason, never makes the movie.

- January 18, 1923. Immensely popular leading man Wallace Reid, the Brad Pitt of his day, dies of a morphine overdose. Four years earlier, while filming *The Valley of the Giants* (1919) in Northern California, he was injured in a train wreck. Not wanting to postpone production, the film company gave him morphine to ease the pain. Insisting that he work even harder to make up for lost time, the company kept supplying him with the opiate until, by the end of production, he was addicted. He dies in a sanitorium in 1923 while trying to detox. His widow, Dorothy Davenport, now calling herself Mrs. Wallace Reid, makes a cautionary film that same year called *Human Wreckage* about the evils of drug addiction.

- November 19, 1924. Producer Thomas Ince dies aboard William Randolph Hearst's yacht *Oneida* under circumstances that remain murky a century after they occur. All that is known is that Ince, newspaper baron Hearst, Hearst's inamorata Marian Davies, Charles Chaplin, Hearst columnist Louella Parsons, novelist Elinor Glyn, and various crew members were present and that Ince was taken off the ship on a stretcher. The official cause of death is given as heart attack, and Ince's remains are cremated before a third party can check it for bullet holes. Since then, the legend has grown that a randy Chaplin was having relations with Davies in one of the staterooms and that Hearst heard about it and entered with a pistol. Hearst shot at Chapin, missed, and hit Ince, who was walking past a porthole, killing him. Louella Parsons knew all about it, and Hearst gave her a lifetime job for keeping her mouth shut. True or not, the speculation fueled a spritely film, *The Cat's Meow* (2001), scripted by Steven Peros from his play and directed by Peter Bogdanovich, a scholar of Hollywood lore.

In the bloody wake of these and other high-profile scandals, public outrage against Hollywood's inability to keep its fly zipped led Congress and nearly three dozen states to debate passing laws against the movies. To prevent such legislation, the heads of the studios gathered in a panic to police themselves, or at least to appear to do so. In a lesson to all who seek to mollify their enemies by compromising before it's necessary to do so, they wound up creating more problems than they solved.

It was a practical decision as well as a political one. With every town having different rules, it was impossible for distributors to know what version of their movies would pass which censorship boards. And because prints were shipped from one town to another as each engagement ended, one city's permissible footage might wind up being another city's offense. There were two ways out: yield to a national film censorship bureau or produce pictures that offended no one. The film companies chose the latter.

On March 10, 1921, the reigning moguls formed the Motion Picture Producers and Distributors of America (MPPDA), a trade (lobbying) organization. Incorporated under the laws of New York, its directors included industry titans William Fox, D. W. Griffith, Lewis J. Selznick, Adolph Zukor, Carl Laemmle, Marcus Loew, Frank Godsol, and ten other men. The paperwork was largely boilerplate corporate language containing such things as protocols for holding meetings, the election of officers, and a mission statement. Appropriate public announcements followed, and Hollywood was applauded for putting its own house in order.

But like so much in Hollywood, looks were deceiving. Not only were there no provisions in the MPPDA incorporation papers for what was and was not to be permitted on the screen, there were no teeth to enforce its decisions. Then, on January 14, 1922, Postmaster General William Harrison Hays accepted an offer from Lewis J. Selznick and Paul Rogers, acting on behalf of the MPPDA, to become the group's president at a salary of $100,000 a year.[7]

Hays looked like he had stepped out of a Grant Wood painting. His ears stuck out like a taxicab with the doors open, he had a mouth like a jack-o'-lantern, and his manner of speaking was straight out of an Indiana cornfield. He was as homespun as one could be, but his most important feature was that he wasn't Jewish. In fact, he was an elder in the Presbyterian Church. As President Harding's postmaster general—a position he was handed as patronage for having run Harding's successful 1920 presidential campaign—Hays exuded tradition and morality.

It was forgotten that he had been involved in the Teapot Dome scandal, which was still making headlines when he accepted the MPPDA post.

"In 1922 when Hays came in as head of the motion picture industry," said producer Hal Roach, "and a very severe code of ethics was placed on the people who made motion pictures, the next year motion pictures increased by 30 percent in attendance." Roach then added, "Will Hays was, first, a very good friend of mine, a very nice man, a very common man. He liked a joke. He didn't drink. He didn't smoke. But, outside of that, he was very human. But he was dedicated to the industry and probably did more good for the industry than anybody else I can think of."[8]

On June 24, 1924, yielding to continued public pressure, the Association released a statement reiterating its promise to avoid objectionable material on the screen. The statement was nothing short of word salad that vowed not to produce salacious or misleading novels or plays but said nothing about original screen stories.

Things got serious in 1927 for the Hays Office,[9] which is what the MPPDA's division, the Production Code Administration, was being called by the time talkies arrived, when an agreement was executed among the Authors' League of America, the Dramatists' Guild of the Authors' League, the Authors' Guild of the Authors' League, and the Motion Picture Producers and Distributors of America, Inc. Signed on December 15, 1927, it included four appendixes, which contained details of what was and wasn't to be allowed on the screen. Appendix C contained the mechanics by which members would notify one another when they purchased a property. Appendix F restated the reasons for the agreement. But it was the other appendixes that held the devilish details.

Specifically, Appendix D was a roster of "Don'ts and Be Carefuls" that listed words, images, and ideas that would not be tolerated. Irony of ironies, it was so specific that the list itself couldn't be read on the screen. Appendix E expanded the list, applying them to "talking, synchronized, and silent motion pictures." The list was so lurid that it could never, under its own provisions, be read or shown on the screen (see this book's appendix). The irony was probably not lost on two men who, while they had a high profile in Hollywood, kept a low profile in this one instance. They were trade paper publisher (*Motion Picture Herald*) and Catholic layman Martin Quigley[10] and Jesuit priest Daniel A. Lord, who were the secret scribes behind what became the Production Code.

Enforcement in these early days was spotty. Producers and distributors had to submit their finished films to the Production Code Administration for a Code seal if they were to be released, or—and this was the escape clause—they had to pay a fine of $25,000 if the film was released without a Code seal. If they wished, they could appeal the decision to a committee made of the other member companies that included, by definition, their competitors. Like manufacturers over the years who found it cheaper to pay fines than fix their faulty products, the studios could absorb the extra costs as part of their overhead. No companies dared use this escape clause, however, fearful of public reaction. It should also be noted that the MPPDA and Production Code Administration was funded by producers who had to pay not only a membership fee but also a separate fee, on a sliding scale, for each film that was reviewed.

Nobody cared because movies were minting money. The Great War may have failed in its goal of making the world safe for democracy, but it strengthened Hollywood by virtually destroying European film production. Even when the Great Depression hobbled the American economy, movies were still riding high as people eagerly spent their quarters to sit in the dark and have their dreams restored.

This apparent financial invulnerability did not go unnoticed by certain forces who viewed the consolidation of theatre chains and film production companies with alarm and began a pressure campaign against Hays and the "shrewd Hebrews" who ran the movie business. Realizing that the industry's most vulnerable spot was not its monopolistic business practices (that would come in 1938) but its owners and screen content, Hays was motivated to move forward on self-censorship.[11]

By the time the Depression inevitably hit Hollywood and the studios had to tighten their belts, they had discovered a formula for commercial success in what are now called "Pre-Code films," pictures that flouted morals, glorified violence, and gave a hurting public entertainment that didn't mind its manners. Many of these films seemed to use the Hays Code's list of "Don'ts and Be Carefuls" as story points and dialogue. Viewed in hindsight, the best of these films crackle with edgy dialogue and sensationalist situations, although some scholars dispute that they were racier than post-Code fare. The MPPDA Digital Archive, in an unsigned entry, explains that it wasn't the films; it was their advertising that raised eyebrows: "Certainly the commonly-made assertion that the Code was not applied during this period, or was applied only ineffectually, is quite without foundation, and to describe the movies of these years as a 'pre-Code' cinema is completely inaccurate. The early 1930s was, however, a period of moral conservatism in American culture and elsewhere, and both the SRC (Studio Relations Committee) and state censors applied increasingly strict standards. The industry's most vociferous critics judged the movies on their advertising far more frequently than on their content."[12] Indeed, one film, 1933's *Convention City*, was touted with the advertising slogan, "Why 1,000,000 men leave home every year . . . to go to conventions. See how they pet and play and pay while wifey is far away." Historian William K. Everson said that this was the film that almost single-handedly brought on the Production Code[13] and, in fact, was considered so scurrilous that Jack L. Warner ordered the negative and every print destroyed, making it the Holy Grail of today's film scholars.

The Hollywood party (which coincidentally was the title of another pre-Code film) was over on June 13, 1934, when Joseph I. Breen was hired by Hays at $60,000 a year plus perks to put teeth in the Production Code Administration. It was exactly the dentistry that Hollywood feared.

2

JOE BREEN

Before turning the Hays Office into the Breen Office, Joseph Ignatius Breen had been a publicity man for Hays released to the MPPDA office in California. In actuality, he was posted there to keep a closer eye on the industry. He was Hays's hatchet man, and his appointment as enforcer of the Code was a brilliant choice. Born in Philadelphia, the son of fiercely Irish parents, he attended St. Joseph's College but left after his sophomore year to become a reporter. A Catholic scholar and a firebrand of a man, Breen took note of the 1933 formation of the Legion of Decency and modeled the Production Code to align with Catholic doctrine. What was little known at the time is that, while working at the MPPDA, Breen also organized nationwide protests within the Catholic community against the MPPDA's own members. When Breen was made head of the Production Code Administration, it was less a sense of competition with the Legion of Decency than of consolidation.[1]

One of his first acts was to decree that no film could be exhibited in the United States without a Code seal and to repeat that any company failing to obtain one would be levied the $25,000 fine that would now be enforced. Moreover, a Code seal would not be given to any film that did not adhere to the "Don'ts and Be Carefuls." It soon became apparent to Hollywood that, rather than wait until their films were finished to submit them to the Breen Office, it would be more efficient to send Breen's people the book, treatment, or screenplay before taking them before the camera. In First Amendment terms, this would be called "prior restraint," but within privately run Hollywood, it was simple efficiency. On July 1, 1934, MPPDA signatories began thirty-four years of chess with a man described by *Liberty Magazine* in 1936 as having "more influence in standardizing world thinking than Mussolini, Hitler, or Stalin."[2]

One troubling aspect of the Hays Office had been that, when it began, one of its provisions was that the written correspondence that passed between it and the studios would not be open to public scrutiny. "Censorship is a dark and dirty business," declared Gerald Gardner, who gained access to that correspondence. "Virtually all of these letters are signed by Joseph E. [*sic*] Breen, the likable, protean head of the censorship board. . . . Doubtless many of the letters that bore his signature were written by one of his assistants—the erudite Geoffrey Shurlock, who would one day succeed him, the witty Jack Vizzard, who would one day write an incisive memoir of his censoring days, and the rest. The censors wanted to imply that they spoke with one voice, and so Breen signed all the correspondence. In a larger sense, the voice was that of Will Hays, the Hoosier politician who had come to Hollywood to keep the government off the filmmakers' backs."[3]

Speaking to the Universal newsreel after his ascension, a bespectacled Breen, meticulously dressed in a three-piece suit and looking squarely into the camera lens, announced unequivocally (while not reading from a script), "It may interest you to sit with us at a meeting of the Production Code Administration in Hollywood where we are working for finer and better motion pictures. Our job as I see it is quite simple. Nobody expects us to, when polled among the public, [make] motion pictures which are lacking in vitality and vigor. No intelligent person would argue that we are to make pictures that are only for children. We must have stories with power and punch and backbone. At the same time, we must be on the lookout for scenes or action or dialogue that are likely to give offense. The responsible men in this industry want no such pictures and will not allow these to be shown. You will understand that our Production Code Office is not a one-man censorship. It represents the considered judgment of many persons of wide experience and a sincere interest in making motion pictures. From the very beginning of the picture, we work with producers, authors, scenario writers, directors, and all who are connected with the production to the end that the finished product can be free from reasonable objection and that our pictures may be the vital and wholesome entertainment we all want these to be." He also said with equal determination, "All motion picture production companies in the United States have joined hands in what has come to be known as a production code of ethics. Its broad, general purpose is to assure screen entertainment which will be reasonably acceptable to our patrons everywhere—entertainment which is definitely free from offense. We must be on the lookout for scenes or action or dialogue which are likely to give offense. The responsible men in this industry want no such pictures and will not allow these to be shown." His final flourish sealed the fate of pre-Code Hollywood: "The vulgar, the cheap, and the tawdry is out. There is no room on the screen at any time for pictures which offend against common decency, and these the industry will not allow."

Breen consolidated the original list of generic "Don'ts and Be Carefuls" that had been adopted by the California (Producers') Association on June 8, 1927, and began enforcing them to the point that they controlled the fate of every film produced and released in America. Independent filmmakers who sought access to theatres also had to get a Code seal. Even after Hays retired in 1945 and was replaced by Eric Johnston, former president of the U.S. Chamber of Commerce, the tenets of the Code remained implacable.[4]

"The producers' code," said Sam Marx, who was story editor at MGM at the time, "which, believe me, I, as a story editor, had to adhere to . . . was torture at times. We did ridiculous things."[5]

Among things that were subject to scissors were kisses that lasted longer than five seconds and any suggestion of a toilet in the bathroom. Couples—even if married—had to each keep one foot on the floor at all times if they were in bed. Stories are legion of films that underwent self-censorship under Breen's and his underlings' blue pencils: *Casablanca, The Treasure of Sierra Madre, Pal Joey, The African Queen, A Night at the Opera, The Letter,* and even *Bedtime for Bonzo,* not to mention *Gone with the Wind* and *The Outlaw.* The correspondence is on file at the Margaret Herrick Library of the Academy of Motion Picture Arts and Sciences.[6] Many are at times picayune, outrageous, helpful, imperious, fanciful, and, in hindsight, bizarre. But they also reveal that Joe Breen was an articulate, diplomatic, and stunningly literate administrator. This was a man, albeit an ideologue, who truly wanted to ease the creative process on the one hand and keep Hollywood safe from government repression on the other. A reading of just a handful of his exquisitely detailed letters is impressive as well as frustrating to those who know the finished films.

These examples are by no means exhaustive but show Breen's (and his staffers') urbanity, tenacity, and eagle eyes:

The Treasure of the Sierra Madre (1948)

Rather than focus his concern on sex (although Breen did gently caution Jack Warner against allowing any notion that Mexican women appearing in the film were prostitutes), he was more concerned that the film not portray Mexicans, as a whole, in an unfavorable light.

The African Queen (1951)

Breen cited the entire relationship between Rosie (Katharine Hepburn) and Charley (Humphrey Bogart) as immoral based on the James Agee script. He also expressed concern that "Negroes seem to resent the appellation 'black,'" that Robert Morley's parson character should be presented with respect, and that no natives should be shown naked.

High Noon (1952)

The quintessential "one man against the world" western produced by Stanley Kramer and directed by Fred Zinnemann did not escape Code scrutiny. The Catholic Breen was concerned about the portrayal of Amy's (Grace Kelley's) Quaker beliefs, specifically in the way she picks up a gun at the end and kills one of her husband's (Gary Cooper's) antagonists. "We think it is essential that you secure adequate technical advice concerning the characterization," Breen wrote Kramer on August 14, 1951, "in order to avoid offending the religious sensibilities of the Society of Friends." Somehow Breen must have been mollified, because the film indeed ends that way and went on to win the Academy Award. Breen was also mindful that Helen Ramirez (Katy Jurado) appears to be

Harvey's (Lloyd Bridges's) mistress and suggests dodging that appearance by suggesting that "she was perhaps engaged to marry these several men in the past . . . eliminating the definite indication that, with each of these men, she had been engaged and is engaging in an illicit sex affair."

Casablanca (1942)

The most important thing to remember about *Casablanca* is that, when they were making *Casablanca*, nobody knew that *Casablanca* was going to be, well, *Casablanca*. In the original script by Julius and Philip Epstein (which Howard Koch took over when the Epstein twins were called away), Captain Renault (Claude Rains) made no secret that he traded exit visas for sexual favors from women. Now it is only hinted at, and Rick (Humphrey Bogart) strategically refuses one such deal in the planning stage.

"We have received one of the incomplete scripts[7] for your proposed picture *Casablanca*," Breen's letter to Jack Warner of May 1, 1942, began. "While we cannot give you a final opinion until we receive the balance of the script . . . going through the material so far submitted, we call your attention to the following:

"Page 5: The following lines seem unacceptably suggestive . . . 'Of course, a beautiful young girl for Monsieur Renault, the Prefect of Police.'

Page 14 : . . . The following lines seem unacceptably suggestive: 'It used to take a villa in Cannes . . . and a string of pearls. Now all I ask is an exit visa.'

Page 38: The following dialogue seems unacceptable: 'How extravagant you are, throwing away women like that. Some day they may be rationed.'" *Rationed* was changed to *scarce*. Go figure.

On June 18, Breen even became a screenwriter, suggesting changes to the flashback scene between Rick and Ilsa (Ingrid Bergman) in Paris:

"The present material seems to contain a suggestion of a sexual affair which would be unacceptable if it came through in the finished picture. We believe this could possibly be corrected by replacing the fadeout [of Rick and Ilsa cuddling] with a dissolve, and shooting the succeeding scene without any sign of a bed." Of course, it was important for Ilsa to think that Victor was dead, not merely out of town, while both she and France were occupied.

Citizen Kane (1941)

The original script by Herman Mankiewicz (if you believe Pauline Kael) or by Mankiewicz and Orson Welles (if you believe Peter Bogdanovich) had a scene in a brothel just after Charles Foster Kane (Orson Welles) has hired away the staff of his competing newspaper, the *Chronicle*, to work on his paper, the *Inquirer*. Surely Welles and Mankiewicz knew that the Breen Office would never permit a whorehouse on the screen, but, like savvy screenwriters, they used it as a bargaining chip, figuring that Breen would kill the blatantly offensive scenes and leave the lesser ones alone.

"There is one important detail in the story at hand," Breen wrote Joseph Nolan, RKO's production representative, on July 15, 1940, "which is quite definitely in violation of the Production Code and, consequently, cannot be approved. This is the locale, set down for Scene 64, which is, inescapably, a brothel. Please have in mind that there is a specific regulation in the Production Code which prohibits the exhibition of brothels."

After "going through the script page by page," Breen raised comparatively minor hackles over scenes of drinking and drunkenness, implying that Georgie, the woman in the brothel, is a madam; removing *Lord* from Kane's speech, "Lord only knows"; and stopping a reporter from patting a Xanadu statue on its tush.

Duel in the Sun (1946)

Producer David O. Selznick's ambitious attempt to supplant *Gone with the Wind* from the lead in his eventual obituary met with a firestorm of protests from the Breen Office. The sprawling story of a Mexican woman (Jennifer Jones) menaced by an evil cowboy (Gregory Peck) went through countless rewrites while it was in production in 1944, some of them by Selznick himself. These would be delivered to director King Vidor (before he walked off the picture) wet from mimeo in the morning before they had been cleared by the Code. Breen was not pleased with this process and engaged in an extraordinary correspondence with distributor RKO's William Gordon, Selznick's Margaret McConnell, and, finally, Selznick himself. Breen's trust in Selznick's observance of the Code was so lacking that he reportedly dispatched Geoffrey Shurlock (who would inherit Breen's job a decade later) to the Tucson desert location to ensure that Miss Jones's costumes were not too revealing. Among points raised in the Breen–Selznick exchanges:

> Showing a hanged man's legs kicking in the air
>
> The suggestion that Peck rapes Jones
>
> The dialogue "I get that kind of service from my studs"
>
> "A river bathing sequence must not show men and woman nude"

The sequence of the mating of the horses

The characterization of men of the cloth

"There is something immoral about the manner of the conversation by the two brothers while Jennifer Jones is crying her heart out after being raped"

And finally, in the shoot-out that ends the film, "For the *Duel in the Sun* climax, this is correct as a payoff on what has preceded it, except at the very finish, wherein Peck kisses Jones and dies. In this way, they both not only get what they deserve, but what they want, and [it] actually amounts to a scene of sublimation and exaltation."

While most producers obeyed Breen, Selznick knew that he had wiggle room. Five years earlier, the men had resolved the problem of Rhett Butler's famous exit line in *Gone with the Wind* with mutual chicanery. While everyone agreed that the use of the word *damn* in "Frankly, my dear, I don't give a damn" was appropriate, the Code dictated otherwise. To save face, Selznick and Breen agreed to allow the word but that it would cost the producer a $5,000 fine.

Thus, in *Duel in the Sun*, Selznick ignored some of Breen's orders while instituting others. It hardly mattered given the chilly reception that the overheated film received from press and public (who called it *Lust in the Dust*), and David O. Selznick went to his grave in 1965, as he feared, celebrated as the producer of *Gone with the Wind*.

The Outlaw (1943/1946)

They say that nothing is dirtier than the mind of a censor, which made Howard Hughes's notorious production *The Outlaw* a litmus test of the

Breen Office. Their tug-of-war over this putative retelling of the Billy the Kid legend is worthy of its own book. In reality, however, it is more about the passion of its producer and financier, Howard Hughes, to share his erotic fantasies with the public than it is of its story about a horny teenage gunslinger. It's interesting to note that Breen's cautions about female exposure are particularly prescient in that he did not know at the time he wrote his cautions that the female being exposed would be Jane Russell.

Hughes intended to release *The Outlaw* through United Artists. Breen's December 27, 1940, response to Hughes's script began with his oft-repeated yet diplomatic notice that "the present version seems to contain various elements which seem to be in violation of the Production Code and whose inclusion in the finished picture we believe would render it unacceptable." It might be argued that the things Breen found objectionable were the same ones that compelled Hughes to want to make the picture in the first place:

"Billy the Kid is characterized as a major criminal who is allowed to go free and unpunished;

"Great care will be needed in [the] scene of the struggle between Billy (Jack Buetel) and Rio (Jane Russell) in the hayloft to avoid any questionable angles or postures;

"Care will be needed in [the] scene of Billy pulling Rio down on the neck and kissing her, to avoid sex suggestiveness."

One testy exchange between Hughes and Breen involved Hughes's dialogue "You borrowed from me, I borrowed from you." When Breen strangely suggested replacing it with "How about tit for tat," Hughes gleefully flew with it and never looked back.

When Breen finally saw the finished picture on March 28, 1941, he was not happy, to say the least, and his response to Hughes is a model of dry Irish wit. "As you know," he began, "we had the pleasure this afternoon of witnessing the projection room showing of your production titled *The Outlaw*. . . . [It] is definitely and specifically in violation of our Production Code and, because of this, it cannot be approved." He ended it with a vague but suggestive understatement: "Before this picture can be approved all the shots of the girl's breasts where they are not fully covered must be entirely deleted from your picture."

Just to make sure he had God on his side, Breen wrote Will Hays, who was still president of the MPPDA, about the preponderance of women's breasts in an increasing number of films. "The practice has become so prevalent," he said, "as to make it necessary for us, almost every day, to hold up a picture which contains these unacceptable breast shots." He concluded by writing (in what could have been, had the correspondence gone public, a publicity blurb that would fill every seat for weeks), "Yesterday we had the exhibition of breast shots in Howard Hughes' picture *The Outlaw* which outdoes anything we have ever seen on the motion picture screen."

On April 8, a somewhat calmer Breen wrote a more measured directive to Hughes with details (clearly culled from carefully, if not repeatedly, examining the naughty bits) of how to de-breast *The Outlaw*, insisting, "see just how many of these shots [the cutter] can delete without seriously interfering with your story line." He named reels 5, 6, 8, and 10, "which are the reels in which most of the objectionable breast shots appear," and reel 7, in which "there appear to be eleven or twelve breast shots . . . we direct your attention to the long and sustained scene in which the girl is sitting on the stump of a tree; the bad shot is as she leans over the fire."

After an appeal by Hughes to the MPPDA's Board of Directors, Breen issued a final missive advising that a Code seal would be issued if an additional five changes were made. They were, and *The Outlaw* opened at San Francisco's Gaiety Theatre on February 5, 1943.

Double Indemnity (1944)

Sometimes creative conflict worked to a film's advantage. When Billy Wilder and Raymond Chandler adapted James M. Cain's novel *Double Indemnity* for the screen, they hit a Code impasse. *Double Indemnity* is close in plot to another Cain novel, *The Postman Always Rings Twice* (illicit lovers, murder), that had vexed both Metro-Goldwyn-Mayer and Paramount for a decade, with MGM ultimately making *Postman* after major cleansing. *Double Indemnity* wrought the wrath of the Code while it was still in novel form with Breen advising his Paramount contact, Luigi Luraschi, on March 15, 1946, that, lacking a Code seal, no exhibitor in America would show it. "As we read it," the missive began, "this is the story of the murder of a man by his wife and an insurance agent who is apparently her lover. The motive of the murder is to collect insurance on the dead man, which the murderous couple had conspired to place upon his life. At the end of the story, the crime is confessed by one of the murderers to the auditors of the insurance company, who proceed thereupon to withhold this information from the proper legal authorities and successfully effect a gross miscarriage of justice by arranging for the escape of the two murderers." Among other objectionable points was the explicit planning of the murder. Paramount ignored Breen's concerns and sent him a script-in-progress, causing him to respond, on September 24, to make sure that Phyllis's (eventually Barbara Stanwyck's) bath towel extends beneath her knees and to remove dialogue suggesting that the wearing of gloves would reduce the risk of fingerprint identification (apparently fingerprint ID was an FBI secret at the time). When he was sent the shooting script in November he wrote, on December 1, that the sequence in the gas chamber was too explicit and should be cut, which it was, but only after it had been shot and reconsidered.

It might be suggested that, by having their hands tied, Wilder and Chandler invented a more poetic and satisfying ending than Cain had put in his novel. Likewise, it might be generously said that Breen's iron fist inspired other filmmakers to playfully obey the letter of the law while evading its spirit. In fact, this became something of a game among experienced writers and directors who flew just under Breen's wire. Typical is this exchange in Howard Hawks's *His Girl Friday* (1940; screenplay by Charles Lederer from the Ben Hecht–Charles MacArthur play *The Front Page*):

Hildy Johnson: What was the name of the Mayor's first wife?

Walter Burns: The one with the wart on her—

Hildy Johnson: — Yes—

Walter Burns: — Fanny.

Or—Hawks again—in *Bringing Up Baby* (1938) when paleontologist Cary Grant is asking his female assistant where to place a bone in the dinosaur skeleton he is reconstructing:

David Huxley: Alice, I think this one must belong in the tail.

Alice Swallow: Nonsense. You tried it in the tail yesterday and it didn't fit.

Here's an exchange from *The Front Page*, the 1931 film that predated *His Girl Friday*:

Reporter #1: An old lady just phoned the detective bureau and claims Earl Williams is hiding under her piazza.

Reporter #2: Tell her to stand up.

Or the famous last moments in Alfred Hitchcock's *North by Northwest* (1959) where Cary Grant pulls his new wife, Eva Marie Saint, into the upper berth of their sleeping car followed by a Freudian shot of a train entering a tunnel.

Not every Code dodge starred Cary Grant. The Three Stooges, of all people, had a map in one of their two-reelers that showed the "Giva Dam." Screenwriter Gore Vidal advised actor Stephen Boyd in *Ben-Hur* (1959) to play the Roman tribune Messala as if he was in love with Charlton Heston, "but don't tell Chuck." Cecil B. DeMille in his biblical epics routinely condemned sin, but only after being sure to show exactly what kind of sin he was about to condemn. And for every line of Groucho Marx that got cut from *A Night at the Opera* (1935; Margaret Dumont: "Rufus, do you have everything?" Marx: "I haven't had any complaints yet"), he got away with another one in *Duck Soup* (1933; "Remember, you're fighting for this woman's honor, which is probably more than she ever did").

Did audiences listen between the lines? Of course they did. But it was Breen's job to make the space between the lines so thin that only adults, at best, could hear.

Was Breen a humorless ideologue? Only in public. In the office, according to Jack Vizzard, he knew the world was round. Yet he had so little respect for filmmakers that he told Vizzard, who questioned the specificity of the "Don'ts and Be Carefuls," "They'd put fucking in Macy's window if you gave them a chance and they'd argue till they were blue in the face that it was art."[8]

Considering that he had the power to render an entire industry's product unsuitable for public consumption—and to do it under the authority of that same industry—Breen was studiously evenhanded. Unlike today's MPAA, whose Ratings Board is constantly under fire for holding independent films to a tougher standard than studio releases, Breen cut no one any slack. Vizzard, who worked under him from 1944 until Breen's retirement ten years later, himself retiring when the Code died in the late 1960s, offered an insider's colorful perspective in his 1970 memoir *See No Evil: Life Inside a Hollywood Censor*.

"I had a purpose, all right," Vizzard writes (sarcastically, one hopes) of wanting to work for the Production Code Administration. "I was rushing down out of the theological hills to save the world from those goddamn Jews." He recalls that Breen, unlike the defender of decency he embodied on the job, could fling as good as he got. When he once presented Harry Cohn, the tough-talking head of Columbia Pictures, with a list of his studio's transgressions, Cohn barked at Breen, "What's all this shit?" Breen responded, "Mr. Cohn, I take that as a compliment."

"What does that mean?" Cohn challenged.

"My friends inform me," Breen said, "that if there's any expert in this town on shit, it's you. So if I have to be judged, I'm glad it's by professionals."

Vizzard reports on a compromise that a producer reached with Breen that showed his boss's pragmatism. A film contained twenty killings, and Breen, through his staffer Charley Metzger, set the limit at ten. A conference was arranged with the producer, who argued that his film needed that many killings and that they should be kept in for "extenuating circumstances." What kind of circumstances? Explained the producer, his wife had a lot of relatives, and she wanted them all to be given jobs on her husband's film. The only way he could do it was to hire them all and have them killed by the end of reel three so as not to interfere with the plot. This was something that Breen, who had six children of his own, could relate to. He gave the film a Code seal.[9]

He was also uncorruptible. When a new Cadillac wrapped in ribbons appeared in his driveway one Christmas morning, he tore the "To/From" card off the bow and called the head of the studio who gave it to him, demanding that it be removed immediately. Breen applied his morality to himself as well as the pictures he censored.

There was only one time when Breen met his match, and it wasn't Howard Hughes (who not only could have taken over any of the studios that paid Breen's salary but did: he bought RKO in 1948).

It was Otto Preminger.

3

OTTO PREMINGER

Otto Preminger was a walking publicity magnet. Teutonic, confident, argumentative, and principled, he had an instinct for headlines. When he shot a movie, he didn't care how many actors' egos he crushed (supposedly he once fired leading actor Tom Tryon from *The Cardinal* in front of the star's visiting parents). When he bought a bestseller for the screen, he angered authors by saying he had no responsibility to adapt it faithfully. He browbeat his staff, tormented studio bosses, and courted the press. He was known as a tyrant on the set, hectoring Liza Minnelli mercilessly on *Tell Me That You Love Me, Junie Moon*, and invariably conjured an image as the successor to Erich von Stroheim as "the man you love to hate" ("I have to be nice to Otto," Billy Wilder once said, "because I still have family in the old country"[1]).

And yet, in a social setting, he could be a charming, generous man. He collected paintings, drank fine wines, supported noble causes, and took care of maître d's the world over.

In his directing career, however, he was obdurate. His insistence on the possessive credit for his films, even though he never wrote them, became such an obsession that director Burt Kennedy, who, unlike

Otto, did write his own films, once joked, "I passed Otto Preminger's house last night. Or is it 'a house by Otto Preminger'?"

Preminger was a producer first and a director second, though auteurists find treasures in his widely varied filmography. Wrote Andrew Sarris, "His enemies have never forgiven him for being a director with the personality of a producer,"[2] and there is at least one scholarly article that waxes so passionately about his oeuvre that its praiseful incoherence is howlingly funny.[3] But love him or hate him (the camps are equally divided), you couldn't ignore him. And that was the whole point.

Born in 1905 in a region of Europe that was then Austria-Hungary but is now Ukraine, Otto Ludwig Preminger was raised to follow his father, Markus, a prosecutor, into the practice of law. He had a younger brother, Ingo, who later became an agent and then a producer of two films: *M*A*S*H* (1970) and *The Salzburg Connection* (1972).

Eastern Europe was not hospitable to Jews in the years surrounding the Great War. When Russia invaded the Preminger homeland in 1914, Markus took the family and fled to Austria, thinking it safer. There, Markus Preminger resumed his career as a prosecutor and placed young Otto in a Catholic school where he was indoctrinated with Catholicism. Similarly, Markus was offered a job in the town of Graz, where he was told he would have to convert. He refused and quickly moved the family to Vienna.

By 1923, teenage Otto had veered into theatre, where he fell under the tutelage and thrall of impresario Max Reinhardt. He became an actor, director, and producer, venturing to Broadway in 1935 to direct *Libel*. Darryl F. Zanuck of Twentieth Century-Fox took note and summoned him to Hollywood, where an uncharacteristically compliant Preminger was content to direct whatever script the mogul handed him.

Once he learned how the town worked, however, Preminger balked at being told what to do and was fired. He returned to Broadway in 1939 and both directed and starred in *Margin for Error*, playing a Nazi. Despite being Jewish, the characterization stuck (the accent, bearing, and, later, shaved head helped), and he made his way back to Fox to play another Nazi in *The Pied Piper* in 1942, then to both act in and direct the screen version of *Margin for Error* (1943), which also starred Milton Berle (the mind reels).

Regaining Zanuck's confidence and patronage, he was anointed producer and handed *Laura* (1944) while Zanuck went off to fight in World War II.[4] As soon as the boss was overseas, Preminger fired *Laura*'s director, Rouben Mamoulian; promoted himself director; and reshot his predecessor's footage. *Laura* became a hit, Zanuck forgave him, and Preminger's directing career ascended. He would continue to turn out one or two films a year until his Fox contract ended in 1953 after doing some uncredited retakes for Delmer Dave's *Treasure of the Golden Condor*.

He was not without talent or, certainly, ambition. His work on *Daisy Kenyan* (1947), *Whirlpool* (1950), *Where the Sidewalk Ends* (1950), and *Angel Face* (1953) holds up well for what they are: standard studio fare enlivened by a whiff of sensationalism. They also demonstrate an awareness of the elements of genre even when his skill sometimes falls short of hitting the mark. The question then becomes whether he was challenging the rules or was simply unable to follow them. This is where his critics divide. When, for example, in his most productive years (after leaving Fox) he had almost total control of his work, he tended to indulge. The most egregious example of this is his 1960 *Exodus*, an epic about the birth of the State of Israel which, at three hours, feels like it is told in real time. Indeed, at the premiere, comedian and fellow Jew Mort Sahl became so impatient at the film's glacial pace that he finally said, "Otto, let my people go." Another anecdote adds reference to that moment: when Dalton Trumbo was writing the screenplay from Leon Uris's very long book, Preminger would needle the writer by telling him that this scene or that scene "lacked genius" and did not rise to the level of the other scenes. Remarked Trumbo, "Otto, for God's sake, if we have every scene equally excellent do you realize how monotonous this picture's going to be? It will be impossible to sit through. There must be variety."

"Tell you what," Preminger responded with playful self-awareness, "you make them all excellent and I will direct unevenly."[5]

The Trumbo exchange is also notable in that *Exodus* was Trumbo's first screen credit since being blacklisted thirteen years earlier. Preminger publicly hired him despite his HUAC (House Un-American Activities Committee) taint and informed his studio, United Artists, that he was going to do so. "I had lunch with Mr. Krim and Benjamin of United Artists and took them to lunch at the St. Regis and said that I wanted to give Mr. Trumbo [official screen] credit," Preminger explained. "And they said to me, look—and it was very much to their credit—we won't stop you. You have autonomy in your contract if you want to. We won't publicly agree with you for certain reasons but we will not stop you."[6] It was the first rend in the blacklist's hold on Hollywood and, when it was followed by Kirk Douglas's hiring of Trumbo to script *Spartacus*, started its unraveling. Naturally, both Preminger and his film basked in the publicity.

It may have been *Angel Face*, made on loan-out to RKO, that started the legend of Preminger's treatment (rather mistreatment) of actors that would climax with the bullying of his leads in *Tell Me That You Love*

Me, Junie Moon seventeen years later. By this measure, the story behind *Angel Face* is more interesting than the one on the screen, which is about an ambulance driver (Robert Mitchum) who falls under the spell of the dangerous Jean Simmons. Howard Hughes "presented" the film, which means that it was his money that he was allowing Preminger to spend. At first, Preminger declined to do it, explaining that he didn't like the screenplay that Frank Nugent and Oscar Millard had written from Chester Erskine's story. A quickie rewrite by the highly paid script doctor Ben Hecht didn't improve it to Preminger's satisfaction, and he wanted out. Hughes explained his motives. It seems that Simmons was under personal contract to him, but he had grown to dislike her intensely. The contract was up in eighteen days, and Hughes promised Preminger a bonus if he finished before it lapsed.

Under pressure, or perhaps wallowing in Hughes's permission, Preminger treated the cast poorly, especially Robert Mitchum. For a scene in which Mitchum was to slap Simmons, Preminger ordered him to do it for real and ordered take after take. Finally, Mitchum hauled off and slapped Preminger, asking him if that's the way he wanted it done. Preminger immediately tried to have Mitchum fired, but Hughes refused. Preminger vowed to get even.

It took him twenty-two years. In 1975, he was starting to shoot his terrorist drama, *Rosebud*, in Israel. The star was Robert Mitchum. The first day that Mitchum was due to appear on the set, he arrived drunk. Preminger had expected as much (Mitchum's romance with the bottle was no secret in Hollywood) and fired him on the spot in front of the crew, cast, and onlookers. He replaced Mitchum with Peter O'Toole (no stranger to the bottle, either) whom he had on standby, fully awaiting the moment to exact his vengeance on Mitchum as publicly as possible.

Preminger's occasional presence as an actor gave him the public image that other directors, with the almost exclusive exception of Alfred Hitchcock, never achieved in pre–*Cahiers du Cinéma* Hollywood. Following his debut as Nazi Major Diessen in *The Pied Piper* in 1942, the Jewish Preminger made a career of playing people who, if he were still in Germany, would have sent him to the camps. His most notable role in this regard was Oberst von Scherbach in Billy Wilder's 1953 prisoner-of-war camp drama, *Stalag 17*. Occasional television guest-starring roles, such as the memorable Mr. Freeze[7] in the *Batman* series, led to innumerable talk show appearances where he was charming, articulate, and well informed.

Going back, it had been *Forever Amber* in 1947, while he was still at Fox, that may have given Preminger a taste for scandal.[8] The odyssey of a seventeenth-century woman (Linda Darnell) who ascends to nobility while descending into immorality was based on the sensational bestseller by Kathleen Winsor. It had been first scripted by Jerome Cady and then rewritten by Ring Lardner Jr. When Lardner was called before HUAC in October 1947, Zanuck wasted no time replacing him with Philip Dunne.[9] John Stahl began directing but was removed after a month when Preminger took over (this time the decision was Zanuck's).

Fox entered the fray from the moment they announced that they had acquired Winsor's novel. The Catholic Legion of Decency exploded, saying it glamorized immorality. Surprisingly, Zanuck refused to cancel the project. Not until there were public demonstrations (perhaps organized by Breen) did the studio begin negotiations with the legion to see how it could be filmed without receiving the dreaded "C" (condemned) rating. There were even reports of Fox president Spyros Skouras getting on his knees to Monsignor John T. Nicholas of Cincinnati begging for leniency. Compromises (such as a narration) somewhat mitigated the curse, but *Forever Amber* still received a "B" ("objectionable in part for all"). Several weeks after its release, Fox made additional cuts and added a new ending. Surprisingly, the Breen Office had little to say in the matter and were content to let the Legion of Decency be their unofficial proxy.

Preminger was certainly mindful of the brouhaha and the resulting publicity that a little scandal could attract if not for *Amber* (its budget was $6.4 million, and it returned just under $4 million in rentals), then for some other project someday, somewhere, somehow.

Six years later, that project came along. It was *The Moon Is Blue*.

4

THE MOON IS BLUE

More than half a century after it turned Hollywood on its ear, people are still asking if Otto Preminger purposely made *The Moon Is Blue* to break the Production Code. There has been speculation that, like a general or a diplomat, he waited until the time was right to launch his attack. Or was it just chance? Either way, it worked.

World War II had broadened audiences' attitudes, television was narrowing theatres' income, and the Broadway stage was debuting astonishingly mature works by such new playwrights as Arthur Miller (*Death of a Salesman*, 1949), Tennessee Williams (*A Streetcar Named Desire*, 1949), William Inge (*Picnic*, 1953), and William Gibson (*Two for the Seesaw*, 1958). When each of these plays, all of which ran with no hint of censorship, were made into movies, every one of them suffered Code cuts.

One of the Broadway plays that raised eyebrows but not hackles was F. Hugh Herbert's *The Moon Is Blue*, which opened on March 8, 1951, at Henry Miller's Theatre (now the Stephen Sondheim Theatre) and ran for 924 performances. It starred Barry Nelson, Barbara Bel Geddes, and Donald Cook. A lightweight sex comedy, it follows the chaste Patty O'Neill, who meets an architect, Donald Gresham, and blithely agrees to have drinks with him in his New York apartment. David's upstairs neighbors join them: Gresham's ex-fiancée Cynthia and her father, the charming debaucher David Slater. Both Donald and David are determined to get Patty into bed and are disappointed when she would rather lead a discussion group about modern morality. She rebuffs both of them all evening but the next day runs into Donald again, and he proposes marriage.

The play had enjoyed several productions in small theatres prior to being mounted for Broadway, and this is where the Hollywood plot congeals. Although it was produced by Aldrich & Myers in association with Julius Fleischmann, the force behind it was the man who staged it, Otto Preminger. Returning to his theatre roots after his Fox contract ended, Preminger needed to renew his Hollywood clout, and he knew that the best way to do that was through publicity. *The Moon Is Blue* offered ample opportunity, for its dialogue and situations were glib and grown-up without venturing into vulgarity, at least as far as sophisticated New York playgoers were concerned. Preminger persuaded Herbert to reject a Hollywood sale and form a company (Argyle Productions) with him to produce the film themselves. They did and waited for the offers to come in.

But Hollywood was cautious. The Production Code Administration, in particular, felt that, while playgoers in New York were worldly, those in the flyover states (before they were called that) were more conservative. Words like *mistress, virgin, professional virgin, seduction,* and *pregnant* were flashpoints for the Production Code Administration, but what really set them off was the play's flippant attitude toward morality, missing entirely that Patty keeps her virginity throughout and holds Gresham and Slater accountable for wanting to take it. It was the journey, not the destination, that rankled them. Bel Geddes, who could charm her way through such language on the stage, got to declare such truths as "Men are usually so bored by virgins" and "Godliness does not appeal to me." The one that really gave Breen apoplexy, though, was "You are shallow, cynical, selfish, and immoral, and I like you."

When the property was first run past the Breen Office in June 1951, Samuel Briskin was its intended producer, and Paramount was its interested studio. Breen lost no time telling Briskin in a June 16 letter, "This unacceptability arises from the fact that the humor in this play stems, almost entirely, from a light and gay treatment of the subject of illicit sex and seduction. While there is no actual seduction in the story, the general attitude towards illicit sex seems to violate that Code clause which states: 'Pictures shall not infer that low forms of sex relationship are the accepted or common thing.'" Ultimately, Breen would send the same caution to everybody else who wanted to produce *Moon*, including Jack Warner of Warner Bros. in December 1951. Then Preminger and United Artists got involved.

The timing of a film version of *The Moon Is Blue* was perfect. In 1948, the Department of Justice, after ten years of litigation, forced the film companies into a consent decree[1] that made the studios divorce their theatre chains from their production and distribution operations. The deadline for this severance was 1951. Denied their instant cash flow from thousands of box offices and requiring that each film be sold on its own merits instead of as part of a package (by banning "block booking"), the studios were scrambling. Then there was television, which made them panic on top of scrambling. While they devised such showmanship as 3-D, Todd-AO, Cinerama, CinemaScope, and Smell-O-Vision to pry people out of their living room sofas, the one thing they knew for sure would do it—sex—was off-limits thanks to Joe Breen.

One studio that wasn't being upended by the Consent Decree was
United Artists. Founded in 1919 by Charles Chaplin, Mary Pickford,
D. W. Griffith, and Douglas Fairbanks to distribute their immensely
popular films without using the existing companies, they owned neither
studio facilities nor theatres. Although they had been struggling as their
members' popularity dimmed, they had kept afloat by handling other
independent producers' productions. When these film titans lost interest in their own company, in 1951, they sold United Artists to a manage-
ment team including Arthur Krim, Robert Benjamin, and Matty Fox.
The new owners continued the policy of "never owning a camera or a
soundstage" and adopted a filmmaker-friendly policy of never taking a
film away from a director.[2]

It was Krim and Benjamin whom Preminger approached to finance
The Moon Is Blue. He had plans to shoot it in German[3] as well as English (Herbert, like Preminger, was German, okay, Austrian), and United
Artists allotted them $400,000 (with $500,000 in deferred salaries),
enough for a twenty-four-day shoot. The contract insisted on delivery of
a film that could get a Code seal.

By the time Preminger come knocking at Breen's door in December
1952, it was Breen's assistant, Geoffrey Shurlock, who fielded the matter as director of the Production Code Administration. Doctors had
advised Breen to ease up, but the slightly more liberal Shurlock (as he
would later show with *Man with the Golden Gun* q v.) was still loath to
contradict Breen. In a letter of April 10, 1953, they advised Preminger
that he would have to make major changes to six lines or else be denied
a Code seal. (See the related exchange of letters between Breen and
Preminger on pages 48–51.)

On Preminger's appeal to the Board of Governors of the Motion Picture Association of America (MPAA), Nicholas Schenck, president of Loew's, Inc., which owned MGM, said, "I wouldn't let my daughter see it." Eric Johnston, who by then had taken over for Will Hays as president of the MPAA, wrote the filmmaker that "the Board has reaffirmed its firm and wholehearted support of the Code. . . . The Code has nothing to do with 'styles' or changing customs. It is a document that deals with principles of morality and good taste."[4]

Preminger, in full battle mode (and no doubt knowing that the play was so thin that it would tank without the provocative language), told Breen that he had no intention of making changes. "I am not a crusader or anything like that," he said, "but it gives me great pleasure to fight for my rights. If you don't fight for your rights, you lose them. We have not only the right but the duty to defend the right of free expression; because if this right deteriorates, that is the first step to dictatorship, or totalitarian government." Not only that, he added that if he had to, United Artists would release the film without a Code seal.

With rehearsals starting on January 13, 1953, Preminger started casting. Patty was to be played by Maggie McNamara, who had replaced Bel Geddes during the stage run. As he would try with Jean Seberg in *St. Joan* (1957),[5] Preminger cast the novice McNamara hoping to mold her into the actress he wanted. Unlike Seberg, she was compliant. He cast William Holden as Donald Gresham. Holden, on the threshold of superstardom (*Stalag 17*, the role for which he would win the Oscar, had not yet been released when *The Moon Is Blue* was filmed), was happy to defer his salary in exchange for a piece of the potential gross. And the devilishly charming David Niven won the role of David Slater.

What vexed the Breen Office was "low sex," that is, the casualness with which the characters discussed premarital and extramarital relations. The provocative dirty words were a symptom, not the cause. Per the Code, "Pictures shall not infer [*sic*] that low forms of sex relationship are the accepted or common thing." In its humorless naïveté, the Code had considered sex only in the context of drama. Faced with it as the central theme of a comedy, it was adrift. Writes Joseph Egan, Preminger "had been preparing himself for Joe Breen's response for almost a year and a half. He believed he had all the ammunition he needed and, requesting a meeting with Code personnel, lunched with Geoffrey Shurlock and Jack Vizzard during the first week in January [1953]. Preminger had just started rehearsing his cast in preparation for a January 20 start of production."[6]

Working fifteen-hour days, Preminger shot both the English and the German versions, wrapping on February 20. Seven weeks later, Egan reports, he had an answer print to show to United Artists and to the Breen Office. The distributor faced a dilemma. If they released *The Moon Is Blue* sans seal, they would incur a $25,000 fine. Moreover, many theatres would refuse to play an un-Coded film. If they cut it, they would void Preminger's contract.

The Production Code Administration was also caught in a quandary. If they gave the Code even a slight bend and approved the film, they would set a dangerous precedent. Yet if the film scored a hit with the public without a seal, their power would be severely undercut.

United Artists found wiggle room. Preminger's contract called for him to deliver a film that could get a Code seal. To mitigate their exposure, United Artists quietly removed that clause, giving Preminger full artistic control, not to mention culpability. They also resigned from the MPAA and released *The Moon Is Blue* without a Code seal. It was released on June 3, 1953. Most critics loved it, and some 8,000 theatres booked it to bring in a gross of $6 million on that $400,000 negative cost over the course of its theatrical run. Everybody made out well but Joe Breen.

The Moon Is Blue did not arrive without reaction. In addition to its rejection by the Production Code Administration, it was condemned by the Legion of Decency and personally by Cardinals Spellman of New York and McIntyre of Los Angeles, both of whom urged their flocks to avoid seeing it. Speaking in the film's—and freedom of speech's—favor were the National Council on Freedom from Censorship (affiliated with the American Civil Liberties Union) and the *Saturday Review*, whose June 27, 1953, issue held that the picture "does violate the puritanical spirit of the Code, if not the letter" but posed the larger question "of whether American movies are continually to be hamstrung by rules that confine picture themes, picture morals, and picture language to what is deemed fit for children—or for childlike mentalities."[7]

Preminger rode the controversy like a jockey on a Thoroughbred. He publicly challenged the MPAA to let the public see the film to decide for themselves and told *Variety* in their June 10, 1953, issue that "the ban [was] particularly unfair in view of [the film's] approval from the National Board of Review and censorship boards in New York, Pennsylvania, Illinois, and Massachusetts who had passed it."

Predictably, after *The Moon Is Blue* completed its release in 1954, United Artists rejoined the MPAA. They would leave it again two years later over Preminger's 1955 film, *The Man with the Golden Arm*. On June 27, 1961, the MPAA quietly granted *The Moon Is Blue* its Code seal #20017 so it could be sold to television, where children could see it.[8]

Breen finally retired in October 1954. Jack Vizzard, who had worked with him since 1944, offered an insider's perspective in his 1970 memoir: "He did his part in pulling an important industry out of the doldrums. That was not easy, nor should it be disposed of too lightly. . . . Joe Breen could never have been what he was, nor would all his personality have prevailed, had not the times demanded him. He was as much a creature of the moment as a shaper of it. He had come to lead a recalcitrant and chastened people back into Traditional Morality, in order to change the frown of the Great Father in the skies into a smile. In this sense, the Code was a throwback. In the sense that tradition represented much that is sound and everlasting in human nature, it was an advance from a retrogression."[9]

Vizzard's admiration for Breen is not unwarranted, but it is myopic. The Code was born with a fatal flaw, the same one that infects the legions of so-called watchdogs of "family values" that have weaponized American politics. In Breen's case, as with theirs, it was an attempt to impose Christian values on all of America. While the Catholic Legion of Decency was honest about their ratings being intended primarily for other Catholics, the Breen Office was deceitful about it.

The film industry has always had a fascination with religion yet has never been comfortable portraying it; the joke is that the movies are all about Jewish Hollywood telling Protestant America how to be more Catholic. The Code was a furtive way of attempting this. Like the latter-day bastions of morality who seek to impose their beliefs on others, they, like the Code, are doomed to fail if for no other reason than their arrogance and their ignorance of mainstream society and true American values. The more noise they make beating their drums and waving their Bibles, the more they destroy their own credibility. Otto Preminger may have put the first fatal cracks in the Code, but, as when Edward R. Murrow took Joseph R. McCarthy over the coals in his March 9, 1954, *See It Now* broadcast, the demagogue's decline was already well on its way.

Geoffrey Shurlock, Breen's longtime assistant, took over on October 15, 1954. He had secretly felt that the Code was in desperate need of revision but dared not cross Breen. He would have ample opportunity to see just how far the Code could be revised when he, instead of his predecessor, had his own Otto Preminger experience.

SIDEBAR: PLOT OF *THE MOON IS BLUE*

Shades of *Love Affair* (Leo McCarey, 1939), Patty O'Neil (Maggie McNamara) meets architect Donald Gresham (William Holden) on the observation deck of the Empire State Building. Although only twenty-two, Patty has a refreshingly practical outlook on life. She's not a cynic like Gresham, but her openness attracts him. Gresham invites her to dinner at his apartment. No fool, Patty asks Gresham up front if this means he wants to seduce her. She then goes on to tell him proudly that she is a virgin and has no mind to change that status. Appreciating her honesty but in all likelihood trying to find a way around it, Gresham agrees to leave her alone.

Patty offers to cook dinner for the two of them, and Gresham departs to buy groceries. While he is gone, Gresham's neighbor, David Slater (David Niven), drops in. David's daughter, Cynthia (Dawn Addams), used to go with Gresham. Seeing Patty, Slater switches into lothario mode. Patty invites him to stay for dinner.

During the meal, Patty accidentally soils her dress. Gresham offers her his bathrobe. Cynthia gets wind of this and summons Gresham away, leaving her father alone to try to seduce Patty. Slater proposes to her and offers her $600 with no strings attached. She refuses marriage but takes the money, giving Slater an innocent thank-you kiss. Naturally, this is when Gresham walks in.

Patty angrily changes back into her dress to leave, and Slater returns to his apartment. Somehow, Patty's father, a New York Police detective, shows up, sees Patty and Gresham, and punches Gresham's lights out. He takes Patty home.

Patty returns later to apologize to Gresham. Now it's Slater's turn to appear at the wrong time. He thinks that Gresham and Patty are getting it on. When Gresham learns about Slater's $600 gift, he refuses all explanations and demands that Patty leave.

The next day, Patty and Gresham happen to reconnect atop the Empire State Building. He proposes marriage to her, and she accepts.

SIDEBAR: PREMINGER–BREEN EXCHANGE OF LETTERS

Text of Otto Preminger letter to Joseph Breen, April 13, 1953 (on The Moon Is Blue*/Preminger–Herbert Productions letterhead):*

April 13, 1953

Dear Mr. Breen:

This will acknowledge receipt of your letter of April 10th regarding our picture *The Moon Is Blue.*

Both F. Hugh Herbert and I are disappointed and shocked by your decision, particularly when we compare our picture with several pictures[10] in current release which have been approved by the Code Administration.

Following receipt of your first letter of January 2, 1953 we had a luncheon conference with your representatives Mr. Vizzard and Mr. Shurlock. Without discussing any details of your letter, Mr. Shurlock—who was very familiar with our script and with the stage play—stated that he fully realized that a successful screen adaptation of *The Moon Is Blue* must follow the stage play very closely. Mr. Shurlock was kind enough so that that he knew us both to be men of integrity and good taste, and he suggested that we go ahead and make the picture according to our best judgment, submitting the final product to you. Both of us therefore had reason to hope that your final decision and interpretation of the Code would be governed by the overall story line and moral philosophy of the picture. We therefore leaned over backward in making revisions in our script before we started shooting, incorporating several suggestions made in your letter of January 2nd. To mention a couple of instances: The revised scene between Patty and Slater in which it is made crystal clear that he is advising marriage and not an illicit relationship (as he did in the play and the original script); the final scene on the Empire State building where both Patty and Don, discussing Slater, again deplore and condemn his general attitude and character, thereby reflecting the moral attitude of the whole picture.

And this, Mr. Breen, brings us down to that paragraph in your letter which has hurt us more than your refusal to grant us a seal. You say "the picture contains an unacceptably light attitude towards seduction, illicit sex, chastity and virginity." Not only as craftsmen who have served the industry for many years but as members of the community who have never been connected with anything shady, dishonorable, salacious or illicit, we must object to this unwarranted and unjustified attack.

Our picture does not have a light attitude towards seduction, illicit sex, chastity and virginity; on the contrary, it is a harmless story of a very virtuous girl who works for her living, who neither smokes nor drinks, who is completely honest and outspoken, who resists temptation and whose one aim in life is to get married and have children. She achieves this aim in our picture when she meets a young, upright, typical American boy who shares her views and ethics. There are two protagonists who represent the attitude of the picture. Both of them are extremely articulate and, throughout the picture, whenever either one or the other encounters the contrary philosophy of David, who is the antagonist, they slap him down in no uncertain terms. When he speaks kindly about divorce and marriage she tells him soberly "you shouldn't joke about it. Marriage is much too serious." When also kiddingly he speaks of his inability to raise his own daughter properly, the boy says "It's really very tragic." These are but a couple of instances; we could go on indefinitely. There are no scenes of passion in our picture, no scenes of crime or vice. We concede that there is discussion of sex—a topic of somewhat universal interest—but we are both deeply convinced that it is handled in such a way that it cannot conceivably harm those whom the Code was created to protect. As additional evidence, if such be necessary, we can point to two highly enthusiastic preview audiences—one in conservative Pasadena, the other in Westwood. Nobody was shocked. Nobody walked out though many were there with their teenage children. Of four hundred preview cards, almost unanimously superlative in their praise, not one objected to the morality of the picture. On the contrary, a goodly number expressed their hopes that the picture would not be ruined by censorship.

Sincerely,

(Otto Preminger)

Text of Breen response to Preminger April 16, 1953, MPAA letterhead:

This is to acknowledge your letter of April 13 in which you express your disagreement with our judgment concerning the acceptability, under the Code, of your picture, *The Moon Is Blue*.

We are, naturally, regretful that we have both arrived at such widely separated points of view in so serious a matter.

We feel, however, that no good purpose is to be served by entering into a detailed discussion of the arguments you raise in your letter.

Our decision was reached only after the most careful consideration, and represents the unanimous judgment of the entire Production Code staff.

May we again respectfully recommend that the simplest solution to your problem lies in the procedure we have already suggested: that of taking an appeal to the Board of Directors of this Association. They are in a position to give a final decision in the matter.[11]

We appreciate the frankness with which you state your case.

Very Sincerely, Yours,

(Joseph I. Breen)

5

CARMEN JONES (1954) AND THE MAN WITH THE GOLDEN ARM (1955)

Like *The Moon Is Blue*, *Carmen Jones* had played on Broadway[1] without complaint from censors or audiences and, in fact, drew praise for its all-black (African American and Caribbean American) cast. Adapted by Oscar Hammerstein II from Georges Bizet's opera about a fiery woman who won't give up her man and updated to modern-day Chicago, its stage producer, Billy Rose, held on to the motion picture rights and announced that he would finance and produce the film version. When he was unable to get a production going even with Elia Kazan,[2] Rose sold the project to Twentieth Century-Fox, where Otto Preminger would both direct and produce for his Carlyle Productions.[3] Fox would distribute and commit up to $825,000 of the negative cost,[4] and Darryl F. Zanuck would have script approval and final cut (no doubt knowing of Preminger's gambit with *The Moon Is Blue*).[5]

At the behest of Hammerstein, who had generated controversy with the racially progressive plot elements of his and Richard Rodgers's Broadway smash *South Pacific*, Zanuck submitted the script to Walter White of the NAACP. White praised the script but opined that he was opposed in principle to an "all-Negro" show because of his organization's ongoing fight for integration.[6]

While this was in the process, Preminger had to get Code approval for the screenplay, which was written by Harry Kleiner from Hammerstein's book,[7] and this meant going to his old friend Joseph I. Breen. "I am submitting to you the script of Oscar Hammerstein's *Carmen Jones*," Preminger wrote Breen on April 19, 1954, "which will be the basis for a film which I intend to produce in the near future. I would appreciate hearing from you." Ten days later, Breen wrote back acknowledging a conference that he, Preminger, and Fox liaison Frank McCarthy[8] had just had. Both of his complaints had to do with sex: first, that Carmen shows no remorse for her lustfulness and, second, the sexual nature of Hammerstein's lyrics. On three single-spaced pages, he cited objectionable lyrics such as "would like a slice o' sumpin' nice" and "what I got dat man c'n get" and dialogue such as "Only reason she ain't never late is 'cause all the men kick her out soon as they sober up long enough to get a look at her!" After a May 6 meeting with Preminger and McCarthy, Geoffrey Shurlock advised Joe Breen that both men had agreed to make changes.

But not quite. Confiding to Fox president Spyros Skouras in a May 7 memorandum, McCarthy was concerned that if they obeyed the Code and removed all uses of the word *hell*, "we shall be laughed at by all who saw the Broadway show. And, even more important, we shall lose the scan and the flavor of the lyrics." He also acknowledged that esteemed producer Frank Freeman had objected to the use of *hell* in *On the Waterfront*. What would solve it, McCarthy suggested, is if the Board of Directors of the MPAA would amend the Code to allow use of the words *damn* and *hell*, something that had been in the works for two years.[9] On May 14, Darryl F. Zanuck wrote Skouras echoing McCarthy's sentiments. Meanwhile, Preminger and Hammerstein dug in with a May 8 letter to Breen holding that changing the lyric "fight like hell," which had become established in American vernacular, would not be possible. On May 24, Preminger reiterated his position noting that "fight like hell" has been used on television and in popular speech.

What began as a matter of wording escalated into an internecine struggle. On May 28, 1954, Geoffrey Shurlock dodged responsibility for *hell* by repeating what Breen had told Preminger on May 26: that the decision was up to the MPAA Board and its president, Eric Johnston. On June 2, Breen wrote Preminger suggesting that he appeal the word *hell* to the Board before attempting to shoot the film with the word included. Other lyric changes, Breen added in a letter of June 4 to Johnston, were made reluctantly by Hammerstein.

Going over Breen's head worked. On June 9, 1954, W. C. Michel, Fox's New York representative, wired McCarthy, "Board of Directors of Motion Picture Association today sustained our appeal on use of word (Hell) in 'Toreador Song' lyric and therefore Preminger may proceed with lyric as written by Hammerstein."

Carmen Jones went before the cameras. Olga James appeared as Cindy Lou, a worker in a wartime parachute factory. Her sweetheart Joe (Harry Belafonte) is scheduled to leave for flight training the next day, and the two of them want to get married. This is put into jeopardy when Carmen Jones (Dorothy Dandridge), a tempestuous coworker at the plant, tempts Joe, and then Sergeant Brown (Brock Peters) intercedes and sends Joe on assignment, putting his marriage in jeopardy and placing him within reach of Carmen's claws. In a bizarre production decision, Harry Belafonte's well-known singing voice was replaced on the soundtrack by LeVern Hutcherson and Dorothy Dandridge's voice by a then-unknown Marilyn Horne.

Preminger brought the film in under budget at $750,000. It received its Code seal on September 21, 1954, and it was released on October 28, 1954, returning rentals of $9,812,000.[10] *Hell* and *damn* gradually entered the movies just as they had been spoken in real life for decades.

With Breen retired in 1954, Preminger dealt with Geoffrey Shurlock, who had succeeded Breen, when he made his next feature film, *The Man with the Golden Arm*. Nelson Algren, the author of the book on which the movie was based, hated the film. He cashed the check, but he hated it; when he was asked by photographer Art Shay to pose under the marquee of the Chicago theatre playing Otto Preminger's 1955 movie, he said, "What does this film have to do with me?"[11] Algren may have been upset that Preminger changed the ending and tried to claim creative ownership of his novel about drug addiction, but he had to wait in line until the Production Code finished turning purple over the mere existence of *The Man with the Golden Arm*.

The story began some years earlier. Published in 1949 after Algren returned from World War II, *The Man with the Golden Arm* follows Francis Majcinek, nicknamed Frankie Machine, who deals cards for a living and plays the drums. He was wounded in the war and given morphine for pain, turning him into an addict. He and his disabled wife, Sophie, live together tensely in a Polish neighborhood in Chicago. Frankie's addiction ultimately leads him to accidentally kill his drug dealer, and he tries prying the "thirty-five-pound monkey" off his back with the help of a friend, Molly-O. Jailed for shoplifting, he starts using again after his release. Meanwhile, the police pursue the drug dealer's killer and are led to Frankie. He apparently shakes the habit cold turkey in Molly-O's apartment but, in an altercation with police, is shot and wounded. Depressed and alone, he hangs himself.

Despite its morbid story and downbeat ending, *The Man with the Golden Arm* became a bestseller and was optioned in 1949 not by a major studio, as might be expected, but by actor John Garfield through independent production company Roberts Productions, a partnership of Robert B. Roberts and writer-director Abraham Polonsky. At the time, Polonsky was under scrutiny from HUAC for alleged Communist sympathies and would be blacklisted in April 1951 after refusing to testify to the Committee. Roberts and Polonsky commissioned a script from Paul Trivers[12] and enticed hard-nosed filmmaker Robert Aldrich to direct. Then it was off to the Breen Office on February 27, 1950, with the script.

Breen waited until March 7 and wrote back that "a motion picture based upon [the script] cannot be approved." His reason was the Code's prohibition that "the illegal drug traffic must not be portrayed in such a way as to stimulate curiosity concerning the use of or traffic in such drugs." Although the book and script made no bones about the downside of addiction and therefore in no way could have been considered inspirational, Breen cited the Code's absolute ban on the details of drug use. And since "this dope addiction problem is basic to this story, we suggest you dismiss any further consideration of this material for a motion picture to be made within the Code."[13] Something that could not be dismissed was the brilliance of Breen's careful rejection. He never said Roberts shouldn't make the movie. He just said that, if he did, the Code would reject it. In his mind, Breen was not censoring per se, but that was still enough for Roberts to back off.

But not completely, for Roberts then pitched a rewrite to Pandro S. Berman at MGM. Berman, having long ago left RKO, used the tactic of sidestepping Breen and contacted staffer E. G. Doherty of the

Hays Office. Berman asked Doherty what the chances were of making *Golden Arm* into a film, and Doherty told him (copying Breen to respect protocol) that "we could see no possibility" on approving a film about addiction. Breen took over, however, and let Roberts and Berman know unequivocally, "I have read with extreme care the revised script for your proposed production *The Man with the Golden Arm* and it is our considered and unanimous opinion that this story is totally in violation of the Production Code."

Garfield died in 1952 from a heart attack brought on, as many people said, by pressure from HUAC and the people who were running Hollywood's blacklist.

Three years later, Otto Preminger, still flush from having successfully bested Breen with *The Moon Is Blue* in 1954 and *Carmen Jones* in 1955, was still bent on denting, if not breaking, the Code. His agent-brother, Ingo, got some investors to buy the *Golden Arm* rights from Garfield's estate, and Otto took up the gauntlet. Armed with a new script by Walter Newman, Otto submitted it to the Code Administration. By this time, Breen had retired, and his shoes had been filled by Geoffrey Shurlock, his former assistant. Sensing new meat, Preminger asked Shurlock to reconsider Breen's earlier rejection given that drug addiction was a problem and that his film could perform a public service. This placed Shurlock, who was not as inflexible as Breen, in a tough position. When he had come aboard the Code Administration twenty years earlier, he was neither a Catholic nor a censor. On rising to run the show, he vowed that "each story has to be judged individually on the basis of morality and reasonable decency."[14] But he didn't want to contradict Breen, perhaps fearing that an appearance of leniency would trigger a flood of resubmissions.

Meanwhile, Preminger optimistically made plans to shoot his film. He had two actors in mind to play Frankie: Marlon Brando and Frank Sinatra. Each had recently won acting Oscars—Sinatra for *From Here to Eternity* in 1953 and Brando for *On the Waterfront* in 1954.

"When I had about thirty or forty pages of the script ready," Preminger told Peter Bogdanovich, "I gave one copy to Sinatra's agent and one to Marlon Brando's agent—just to give them an idea of what the picture was about. I got a call the next day from Sinatra's agent, who said, 'He likes it very much.' I said, 'All right. I'll send him the rest of the script as soon as I have it.' He said, 'No, no. He wants to do it without reading the script.' I said, 'Fine.'"

Preminger originally had Lewis Meltzer do an adaptation that he found unacceptable. Then he bewitched Nelson Algren himself to convert his novel. When it became clear to Algren that he and Preminger were not on the same page, he left. Preminger finally had Walter Newman write a draft and at some point, as he had on *Angel Face*, asked Ben Hecht to do an uncredited polish.[15]

"Three or four days later, I called Brando's agent and told him I already had somebody else. He couldn't believe me—he thought I was bluffing. That's how Sinatra came to play the part—he made the decision very quickly. And I must say, it was a wonderful experience. I've never enjoyed working with anybody more than Sinatra. All those stories I hear about him delaying a picture, doing only one take and then walking out, I just can't believe." (Perhaps Sinatra had family in the old country too.)

Preminger was riding the tide of change. As Jon Lewis points out in *Hollywood v. Hard Core*,[16] the mid-1950s saw a box office slump. Television was eroding the movie audience but with a shocking exception:

pictures that tackled more mature themes (*A Streetcar Named Desire, A Place in the Sun, On the Waterfront*, and particularly *The Moon Is Blue*), despite being Breened, were still attracting audiences. While Shurlock was pledged to uphold the Code, the Code was also a part of the MPAA,[17] the trade organization (read lobbyist) for a desperate film industry. As Lewis writes, "A more liberal code promised to encourage the production of films that looked and sounded different from the strictly censored programming on television. But it also promised a showdown with the Legion of Decency and the various state and local censorship boards, the very sort of confrontation the Production Code Administration had endeavored to avoid."[18]

Preminger might as well have summoned Breen back from pasture. Unwilling to contradict his predecessor so soon into his own reign and under pressure from U.S. Narcotics Commissioner Harry Anslinger,[19] Shurlock, on July 3, 1955, advised the filmmaker that the new script was still "fundamentally in violation of the Code clause which prohibits our approving pictures dealing with drug addiction."

But then he did something subtle. Shortly after writing the letter, he phoned Preminger. The two men discussed the project, and afterward, Shurlock wrote a letter discussing changes that would have to be made in the script but without actually promising that such changes would make the film as a whole acceptable to the Code. He may not have blinked, but he winked.

Realizing that nothing they could do would gain Code approval, Preminger and United Artists, in the spring of 1955, made the picture anyway. They shot in New York rather than Nelson Algren's Chicago because of what Preminger called "financial reasons," most likely union considerations. In December, they screened the completed picture as a courtesy for Shurlock and received the expected response:

"As we advised you, the picture is basically in violation of the Production Code. Also, for the record, even if the basic story were acceptable, we feel that there would be two minor items in the picture which would need correction. The first of these is the scene of the preparation of the hypodermic needle when the leading man is given his first injection by the narcotics peddler. The second of these unacceptable elements consists of certain shots of the strip-teaser." (This had been mentioned in the earlier Shurlock letter.)

United Artists, having withdrawn temporarily from the MPAA the year before over *The Moon Is Blue*, did so again, this time on December 7, 1956. Also as before, they later rejoined. What was interesting is that the Legion of Decency, which usually moved in lockstep with the Code, did not condemn *The Man with the Golden Arm* but gave it their slightly lesser "B" rating as they had for Preminger's *Forever Amber*. This was the result of the Legion changing its rules (announced in 1957 but under discussion earlier) because they, unlike the Code, realized that they were losing the faith of the moviegoing public.

Preminger had already made his own changes to Algren's book not so much to mollify the Code as to pander to a wider audience. This is what angered Algren. The first change was to turn Frankie from a blond twenty-year-old into the pushing-forty Sinatra, a casting choice that, while solid, made the character more worldly. His wife, Sophie, is not disabled but is only pretending to be in order to scam him. When it comes time to accidentally kill his drug supplier, Frankie is clearly innocent; it's Sophie who pushes him to his death. Where an abject Frankie hangs himself in the book, in the film, he survives and joins Molly-O.

Compared with the grimness that preceded it, this counted as a happy ending.

It was not happy for Algren, who sued Preminger over the director's use of the possessive credit, "An Otto Preminger Film." He also sued over a promised percentage of the returns but reportedly dropped the action because he didn't have the money to pursue it.[20]

The public and press responded to the film, which, on a budget of $1 million, grossed $4,300,000, returning an estimated $2,150,000 to United Artists.[21] More important, it gave the MPAA a wake-up call that the world was changing and that they needed to change with it.

United Artists' second resignation from the MPAA sent the Hays Office spinning. In January 1956, Eric Johnston quickly called a meeting of studio presidents to update the Code's definition of "community standards" and acknowledge that drug addiction was a problem. "Like most bullies," wrote Gerald Gardner, "the rule of life of the censors was 'push or be pushed,' and with United Artists jumping ship, the Production Code was being pushed."[22] In addition to drugs, the Code examined its appeal process and its treatment of abortion, kidnapping, prostitution, and miscegenation. Johnston had come to realize that the Code had to change along with society. In a somewhat vague edict, he declared that depictions of crime would be judged on a case-by-case basis and could, in responsible instances, be approved. *Hell* and *damn* could be approved in proper context if not overused. But the more he seemed to bend, the more cracks he opened in the Production Code itself, although that poison pill of a $25,000 fine still lurked in the shadows for wanton disobedience.

The film's success impressed the MPAA, whose members nominated Frank Sinatra for Best Actor for his portrayal of Frankie Machine (he lost to Ernest Borgnine's *Marty*), Elmer Bernstein's score, the art direction by Joseph C. Wright, and set decoration by Darrell Silvera. None of them took home the Oscar.

On June 14, 1961, the Production Code Administration gave *The Man with the Golden Arm* a belated Code seal, #20011, so, like *The Moon Is Blue*, it could be sold to television. Apparently, nobody noted the irony that both films, which were considered unsafe for adults when they were originally released, were now okay for all ages to watch alone on the home tube.

No matter. Once again, Otto Preminger had outdone the Code and this time, more important, forced it to consider making changes rather than exceptions.

SIDEBAR: SPIDER-MAN DRUG ISSUE

Otto Preminger wasn't the only one fighting a Code over drugs. At Marvel Comics, editor-writer Stan Lee was facing the same intransigence from the Comics Code Authority. Instituted by the Comics Magazine Association of America trade group in 1954 under the leadership/pressure of Magistrate Charles F. Murphy, the Comics Code Authority was to the comic industry what the Production Code was to Hollywood—and for the same defensive reasons. Like the Hays Code, the Comics Code held dominion over comic books in an effort to de-tarnish the publishing industry's reputation following the hysterical book and subsequent congressional testimony of Dr. Fredric Wertham, author of *Seduction of the Innocent*.

Truth to tell, some pre-Code comics truly were as excessive as pre-Code movies. They featured bloody violence, women in revealing poses, supernatural shocks, and sexually explicit artwork. When the Comics Code came along, it put such titles as *Crime SuspenStories*, *Vault of Horror*, and *Tales from the Crypt* (most of them from William Gaines's EC Comics) out of business along with publishers Eastern Color, Toby Press, Star Press, Sterling, and the comic book division of United Features Syndicate. Those that survived (DC comics' *Action Comics*, *Wonder Woman*, *Batman*, etc.) were tamed to the point of monotony. Even though Marvel, which had been around in a slightly different form since 1939, didn't escape Code wrath, it took sixteen years, with the January 1971 issue #96 of *Amazing Spider-Man*, for them to go to the mat.

Spidey had been around since August 15, 1962, although "been around" didn't quite fit his youthful level of sophistication. As Stan Lee recounted to Les Daniels in the comprehensive *Marvel: Five Fabulous Decades of the World's Greatest Comics*, "I got a letter from the Department of Health Education and Welfare which said, in essence, that they recognized the great influence that Marvel Comics and Spider-Man have on young people. And they thought it would really be beneficial if we created a story warning kids about the dangerous effects of drug addiction. We were happy to help out. I wove the theme into the plot without preaching, because if kids think that you're lecturing them, they won't listen. You have to entertain them while you're teaching."[23]

There was just one problem: the merest mention of drugs was against the rules of the Comics Code Authority, just as it had been to the Production Code Administration when Otto Preminger broached the same issue in 1955. Lee's solution, as he told Roy Thomas in *Comic Book Artist* #2, was very close to the one United Artists chose for *The Man with the Golden Arm*. "The Code mentioned that you mustn't mention drugs," he said, "and, according to their rules, they were right. So I didn't even get mad at them then. I said, 'Screw it' and just took the Code seal off for those three issues. Then we went back to the Code again. I never thought about the Code when I was writing a story, because basically I never wanted to do anything that was, to my mind, too violent or too sexy. I was aware that young people were reading these books, and, had there not been a Code, I don't think that I would have done the stories any differently."[24]

Lee wrote a three-part story that was illustrated by Gil Kane and John Romita Sr. Spidey saves a kid on a rooftop who is on drugs and thinks he can fly. Says Spidey, "I would rather face a hundred super-villains than throw my life away on hard drugs because it is a battle you cannot win!" Although the main story is about Harry Osborn Sr. turning back into the Green Goblin, the subplot has Harry Jr. popping pills in despair over Mary Jane Watson's (the name "Mary Jane" is coincidental) leaving him. Spidey/Peter Parker defeats the Green Goblin by showing him his son's peril. Lee achieved in comics what the motion picture Production Code could not conceive of happening on-screen: rather than demonstrate how to use drugs, Lee and his artists showed how *not* to use them.

As time went on, Wertham's methodology was investigated and discredited. Thereafter, he switched tactics and started writing about the benefits of comic fandom, but the public, by then skeptical of his credibility, found little interest in what he had to say. Although he insisted that he had never called for censorship, that was the effect he achieved, as well as setting the media template for politicians, religious leaders, and activist parents to grab attention by coming out against any new trend that kids might enjoy, from rock and roll to video games.

As for the Comics Code Authority, by 2011, many comic book publishers had simply abandoned it in favor of their own rating system, and it had a quiet, non-explicit death.

6

ANATOMY OF A MURDER (1959) AND ADVISE & CONSENT (1962)

With *The Man with the Golden Arm* making box office hay in its 1955–1956 release, Otto Preminger had two notches on his megaphone against the Production Code. While it can't be known if he chose his next project to drive Geoffrey Shurlock farther up the wall, that's what happened when he bought Robert Traver's 1958 best-selling novel, *Anatomy of a Murder*. Based on a sensational (of course) 1952 murder case, Traver knew the intimate details because he had been the defense counsel under his real name, John D. Voelker, before becoming a Michigan Supreme Court justice.

The crime that inspired it took place July 31, 1952, when Lieutenant Coleman A. Peterson shot and killed Maurice Chenoweth in Big Bay, Michigan. With Voelker as Peterson's defense attorney, the plea was entered of insanity by irresistible impulse, a petition that had not been used in the state for more than half a century. The jury bought the plea and acquitted him, only to have Peterson declared sane two days later by a psychiatrist, after which Peterson and his wife divorced. The circumstances of the murder (Peterson thought his victim had raped his wife), followed by the murkiness of the trial in which Mrs. Peterson's

67

reputation was introduced, increased its newsworthiness and, hence, interest in the novel drawn from it.

The lurid details gave Preminger a chance to hold Geoffrey Shurlock's feet to the fire. Unlike *The Moon Is Blue*, where words like *virgin* were used for comic effect, such clinical terms as *penetration, panties, sperm, bitch, sexual climax,* and *spermatogenesis* in a murder trial where rape was involved were essential and deadly serious. This was the perfect test for Shurlock's promise that context would be considered.

Alas, the British-born, presumably more erudite Shurlock did not rise to his own occasion. "As we indicated to you," he wrote Preminger on December 8, 1958, after reading the script, "while the basic story meets the requirements of the Code, the present version contains two scenes of such a clinical nature, discussing rape, that we fear they would prove unacceptable when we came to review the finished picture. . . . The reference to 'sperm,' 'sexual climax,' 'penetration,' etc., seem to us to be hardly suitable in a picture to be released indiscriminately for mixed audiences. It also seems to us that there is an over-emphasis on the words 'rape' and 'panties.'"

To be sure, Wendell Mayes's crackling procedural screenplay included frank discussion of sexual matters in a contentious trial that took up two-thirds of the picture. Seeking to neutralize Code complaints by having the court address the use of mature language, they had the character of Judge Weaver deliver the following caution:

> *For the benefit of the jury, but more especially for the spectators, the garment mentioned in the testimony was, to be exact, Mrs. Manion's panties. I wanted to get your snickering over and done with. This pair of panties will be mentioned again over the course of this trial and,*

when it is, there will not be one laugh, one snicker, one giggle, or even one smirk in my courtroom. There is nothing comic about a pair of panties that resulted in the violent death of one man and the possible incarceration of another.

Ordinarily, such an admonishment would be like telling children in a school health class not to giggle at the mention of a boner, but in *Anatomy*, it worked, just not on the Code Administration.

On January 15, Preminger spoke with Shurlock and Ken Clark of the Code's Washington, D.C., lobbying office. They agreed to several changes that Shurlock confirmed in a letter to the filmmaker. These included altering the expression *knocked up*, using *evidence* instead of *sperm*, saying *relations* instead of *intercourse*, and cutting back on the use of *rape* and *panties*. He ended by offering thanks "for your cooperation in dealing with this somewhat tricky problem" but then folded his arms, so to speak, by closing his letter with the Code's usual qualification: "You understand, of course, that our final judgment will be based on the finished picture." On February 27, Shurlock approved the new script but added (in a strange revelation for someone who worked in the film industry), "we are informed that the word 'schmuck' is an offensive one. We suggest that you check on this, with the idea of replacing it, should you find that it is objectionable."

On April 29, Preminger fired back. He wrote Shurlock that the author of the book advised that the term *penetration*, not *violation*, is the only legally acceptable term for the act in the Michigan legal system and implored Shurlock to withdraw his objection to its use. He enclosed Traver's/Voelker's legal opinion as a backup. Shurlock resisted in a return letter of April 30, saying that hearing the word in court is one thing but hearing it over a theatre's loudspeaker is another and that, besides, local censorship boards would delete *penetration* anyway even if it were used. He referred Preminger to Eric Johnston for further appeal.

The film walks a delicate line in dramatizing the real case in ways that alter the plot but not its sensationalism. Paul Biegler (James Stewart), a small-town lawyer who used to be a prosecutor until he lost reelection, is asked by Laura Manion (Lee Remick) to defend her husband, Army Lieutenant Frederick "Manny" Manion (Ben Gazzara), who has been charged with murdering Bernard "Barney" Quill, a local innkeeper. Manny admits to the murder but tells Biegler it was justified because Quill raped Laura. After Manny claims to have no knowledge of having committed the murder—in an exquisitely written scene in which both men speak in code—Biegler discovers the rarely used "irresistible urge" wrinkle to the insanity defense and decides to use it.

Biegler disguises his courtroom guile with a folksy manner that occasionally causes disruption among spectators and friction with the remarkably tolerant judge (Joseph N. Welch)[1] as well as the prosecution. When local District Attorney Mitch Lodwick (Brooks West) teams with Claude Dancer (George C. Scott) from the state attorney general's office, Biegler starts to lose ground. Despite opposition from the prosecution, Judge Weaver allows the rape of Laura Manion into the record. The claim of "irresistible urge" is allowed, and the jury acquits Manion, but the viewer is left with the distinct feeling that everyone, including Biegler, has been manipulated.

Despite words like *rape, penetration,* and the rest, the word that unexpectedly kindled Code fireworks came from Manion's cellmate, whom the prosecution calls as a surprise witness to challenge the "irresistible urge" defense. The cellmate, whose rap sheet puts the veracity of his testimony into question, says that Manion told him he was playing everyone for suckers and that "when he got out, the first thing he was going to do was to kick that bitch from here to kingdom come."

Bitch was not essential to the film, and Shurlock said so, but Preminger ignored him and still won Code seal #19294 on June 8, 1959. This was not good enough for the City of Chicago, whose censors banned *Anatomy of a Murder* over its use of medical language. Told by the police chief to take out the word *contraceptive* on the grounds that he would not want his eighteen-year-old daughter to hear it, Preminger replied that if he had an eighteen-year-old daughter, he would not only want her to hear the word but to thoroughly understand it.[2] Columbia's lawyers handily won the case by arguing that such terms were in common use in court, and officiating Judge Julius H. Miner had no choice but to agree.[3] After premieres in Michigan, the film went into general release in the United States on July 2, returning admirable rentals of $8 million on a budget of $2 million.[4]

Anatomy of a Murder, produced on a tight budget of $2 million, returned $8 million in rentals to Columbia Pictures.[5] It set Preminger up as an independent producer who could choose his studio. His next film was the epic *Exodus* based on Leon Uris's chronicle of Israel's independence. The filmmaker had different battles to fight in the course of that complex production, but when it was successfully launched, he turned his sights on another inflammatory bestseller that would put a fourth nail in the Code's coffin, *Advise & Consent*.

That one of Hollywood's leading liberals should make a film of a book written by a reactionary conservative shows either how understanding liberals are or how well Preminger thought it would do at the box office. A complex political drama about a highly contentious vote for Robert Leffingwell (Henry Fonda), an Alger Hiss–like nominee for secretary of state, it won the Pulitzer Prize for Allen Drury in 1960 in a similarly contentious vote within the Pulitzer Committee, which wanted Saul Bellow's *Henderson, the Rain King* to win but was overruled by its own Board.

The title is drawn from the constitutional provision that the president shall appoint his cabinet with the advice and consent of Congress. While over the past half century the process has become partisan, when the book was published in August 1959, it was rare for a president to be denied his choice. That's what helped keep the book on the *New York Times* bestseller list for 102 weeks.

Pleased with Wendell Mayes's work on *Anatomy of a Murder*, Preminger had him adapt Drury's talky novel but with an edge that irritated the novelist. As writer Foster Hirsch pointed out, the director, was more interested "in the Senate as an institution able to correct itself"[6] than in exploiting the drama of a sitting president who pushes his nominee. "More important than the outcome of the voting," he continues, "is the method by which the voting was conducted." Indeed, the film dwells almost to the point of distraction on the complex rules of the Senate: where the members sit, how pages distribute daily paperwork, the bell that announces a quorum call, how senators are recognized to speak, and the sickeningly polite way that rival senators address each other on the floor of "the world's greatest deliberative body."

Although Preminger tried to make the film look evenhanded, he did throw in a few nudges, most notably the hiring of Will Geer in a small role as one of the senators. Geer had been blacklisted following his participation in the 1954 independent film *Salt of the Earth*, and, as Preminger had done for Dalton Trumbo on *Exodus*, the director restored Geer's career. (Geer later starred as Grandpa Walton on *The Waltons* TV series.)

Just as the novel reveals behind-the-scenes Senate coatroom dramas about the government, Preminger's first meeting with Shurlock over the script was off the record too. On July 28, 1961, the two men had a meeting about the script in which Shurlock's main concern was its portrayal of homosexuality. He wanted Preminger's assurances, which Preminger gave, that there would be no "swishy" (Breen's term) characters or condoning of the homosexual lifestyle (which the Code still termed "sexual perversion). "For the record," he wrote to the file that day, "we feel that his approach to homosexuality could be basically inoffensive. In discussing the two or three scenes with Mr. Preminger, he assured me that such was the intention."

Unlike the novel, which was designed by Drury to propagate sequels (as indeed it did, four of them), the film removes some of the complexities. In the novel, the president (Franchot Tone) is more involved in covering up his nominee's lies during the nomination hearings. Rather than involve the president in the treachery, he leaves it to obnoxious peacenik Senator Fred van Ackerman (George Grizzard), who has all the manners and integrity of a Trumper. When the president dies during the final vote, the depth of the cover-up is not revealed in the film as it is in the novel, and Leffingwell's fate ends in a tie, which the vice president, suddenly elevated to the presidency, refuses to decide in Leffingwell's favor, determining to name his own secretary of state.[7] In other words, after 139 minutes, Preminger's takeaway is that the Senate (and thus the Republic) can police itself—as long as you don't ask how.

Despite his intentions, many in the real U.S. Senate were upset with the institution's portrayal as a backroom men's club. But by then, the real fight had been won, for Preminger's more substantial victory in *Advise & Consent* was Hollywood's first portrayal of a gay bar. The "602 Club" was a factor in a subplot in which a married senator, Brigham Anderson (Don Murray), is blackmailed by van Ackerman over a homosexual affair he'd had during the war, and to quash it, Anderson goes to the gay bar to confront his former lover, who had slipped van Ackerman an incriminating letter. Clues were laid for the subplot by having Anderson and his wife (Inga Swenson) sleep in twin beds (one aspect of the Hays Code that complemented the situation) and her regret that their marriage had not been "exciting" for him, a code word for sexless. All that remained was for someone to say, "Do the math."

An important provision of the Code was that "sex perversion or any inference to it is forbidden." As Vito Russo wrote in *The Celluloid Closet*, "According to Wendell Mayes . . . it was always Otto's publicity game to break the Code, and he was successful at that game. There were many for whom the time was not yet ripe to do this, and there were also those for whom the time would never come.

"But the ball was rolling," Russo continues. "In the fall [1961] the Motion Picture Association of America said that it would 'consider approving such references in motion pictures if the allusion to sexual aberration was treated with care, discretion and restraint.' Seizing what was obviously the moment, Preminger, ever the showman, used his appearance at a Washington Press Club luncheon in late September to stun the audience by announcing that the industry's Production Code had been changed to permit the tasteful treatment of homosexuality in order that he might be able to film *Advise & Consent*. The MPAA hotly denied that such a change had taken place but, less than week later, on October 3, 1961, it approved the change publicly." It was only a small victory, for, as Russo notably points out, the homosexual character in *Advise & Consent* suffers the fate of almost all prior movie gays: he commits suicide. By adhering to this unwritten rule, on December 12, 1961, the film was given Code seal #20078.

Coincidentally, as *Advise & Consent* was coming to the screen, plans were being made to film Gore Vidal's 1960 Broadway play *The Best Man*, which also had a homosexual subplot involving a political candidate (Cliff Robertson) who may or may not have had a gay affair during the war and his liberal opponent, played by Henry Fonda, who cannot bring himself to use the smear against him. By further coincidence, Franklin Schaffner, who directed the 1964 film version of *The Best Man*, had directed the 1960 Broadway production of *Advise and Consent*. In his foreword to the published playscript of *The Best Man*, Vidal states, "No, I have never read *Advise and Consent*."[8] In Vidal's case, the suspected gay man lived but didn't win the nomination—not because he was gay but because Fonda broke the tie at convention by endorsing a neutral candidate.

Not long after *Advise & Consent*, the MPAA released a far shorter, more elastic—and strategically vague—Code:

1. No picture should be produced which would lower the moral standards of those who see it.
2. Correct moral standards of life . . . should be presented.
3. Laws—divine or natural or human—should not be ridiculed, nor should sympathy be created for their violation.

It was as clear as mud, but it covered the ground, at least until films like *Bonnie and Clyde* (1967) and *The Thomas Crown Affair* (1968) hit the screen. Not in the least pleased in 1962, however, was Martin J. Quigley. Editorializing in his *Motion Picture Herald* that "homosexuality does not represent correct standards of life by any stretch of the imagination," he felt that even so much as showing a gay person favorably would "create sympathy for those who violate both Divine and human law by perverted acts." Quigley died in 1964 having co-fathered both the Production Code and the Legion of Decency, both of which had outlived their once-powerful influence while remaining in business, at least nominally.

It was clear that screen taboos were falling in the face of public maturity, not so much because conservatives were writing letters to the editors but because they weren't going to movies as often as young, more progressive people. It would remain for Jack Valenti, President Lyndon Johnson's former adviser, to drag the Code kicking and screaming into modern times. But Otto Preminger was not out of the picture yet.

7

SKIRMISHES WITH THE CODE

Otto Preminger's adventures with the Production Code didn't begin with *The Moon Is Blue* and end with *Advise & Consent*. Starting with *Laura* in 1944 and continuing through *Hurry Sundown* in 1967 in the twilight of the old Code, he had his less spectacular skirmishes. To be sure, so did other filmmakers, but Otto was always in the forefront, and one can only imagine how the Production Code Administration's stomach seized every time they saw a letter arrive with a return address from 711 Fifth Avenue, the Columbia Pictures building in New York where Preminger had his office.

Preminger was no naïf when it came to the Code, but his first encounter with it had been handled by his studio. In 1944, he was making (or, rather, taking over for director Rouben Mamoulian) *Laura* for Twentieth Century-Fox. A riveting film noir about a detective (Dana Andrews) who becomes infatuated with a woman (Gene Tierney) whose murder he is trying to solve, it was based on the 1943 bestseller by Vera Caspary. Other characters in the film are columnist Waldo Lydecker (Clifton Webb but, at the time, was to be played by Monty Wooley) and Shelby Carpenter (Vincent Price), a leech on Laura's income.

Reacting in a letter of November 2, 1943, to the studio's liaison Colonel Jason S. Joy (who had formerly headed the Studio Relations Committee for the Code in the 1930s), Joseph Breen warned him about portraying Waldo Lydecker and Laura as anyone more than friends,[1] that drinking be minimized, and that a reference to wiping a telephone clean of fingerprints be deleted, among other observations. A revised script was submitted on November 30, and on December 1, Breen had even more complaints about drinking and the suggestion that various characters had been having illicit affairs. More changes, including two new endings, went to Breen on December 22, and on Christmas Eve, he was fine with the cutbacks in drinking but harped again on wiping prints off the phone, as it would show audiences how to avoid detection when committing a crime. Nevertheless, up until June 5, 1944, Breen and Joy were still swapping letters and script revisions. This was getting painfully close to the planned October release considering that the film had yet to be shot.

While the script was being altered, the Breen Office was also in the process of approving Gene Tierney's wardrobe. This was de rigueur where sex played a part in a story and an attractive actress was to portray a love object.

By August 16, the Breen Office was happy, and *Laura* got a Code seal #10088 and was off to theatres for an October 11 premiere in New York, a national release in November, and enshrinement in the pantheon of films noir.

A bizarre sidelight of all the back-and-forth about drinking, fingerprints, and illicit affairs is that nowhere in the correspondence does anyone mention that, at its core, *Laura* is about necrophilia: a man falls in love with a dead woman. This has been noted by critics for years, yet an examination of the entire fifty-eight-page file in the Production Code

Administration archives says nothing of the most disturbing aspect of the story.

While *Laura* was being made, Fox and Preminger were also trying to bring *Forever Amber* to the screen. This was a supreme challenge. Kathleen Winsor's 1944 historical novel about a seventeenth-century girl who sleeps her way up the court of Charles II while never being able to win the man she truly loves was both praised as a story of a strong-willed woman and condemned for being salacious. Of course, it was both. At nearly one thousand pages after having survived five edits by publisher Macmillan (during World War II, when paper was rationed), it became a bestseller and a natural for movies. That year, Fox bought the film rights for $200,000, but it was contingent on getting Code approval, and Fox told Philip Dunne to stand by to adapt it into a movie and John M. Stahl to direct. (Ring Lardner Jr. would also work on the script.) Its atypically large budget was set at $3 million.

A lot would change before *Forever Amber* was released on October 22, 1947, with its budget having blown up to $6.5 million. After thirty-nine days and $300,000 were spent, studio chief William Goetz (substituting for Darryl F. Zanuck, who was off fighting the Germans) fired Stahl and handed the film to Preminger, who, as director and not producer, would have little say in the vicissitudes of the film but had to wrap it as quickly as possible.[2] Yet he still had to follow the Code, which became as byzantine as anything in Winsor's plot.

The jousts began on October 3, 1944, when Fox's Colonel Jason Joy sent a forty-eight-page synopsis to Joseph Breen (beginning "Dear Joe" as when he worked under him) and asked for his judgment on the novel they were considering. Like a shot, Breen wrote back the next day, "Dear Col. Joy" (so much for bonhomie), "it is our considered opinion that this story is utterly and completely unacceptable under any one of a dozen provisions of the Production Code." As if to drive their point home with a tank, someone in the Breen Office planted a story on the United Press International wire that the Hays Office had discouraged any bidding for the novel. That didn't stop the studios from doing so, and on October 19, Breen gave the same negative appraisal to Louis B. Mayer of MGM, who had also submitted the treatment, replying that it is "hardly more than a saga of illicit sex and adultery into which enters the elements, on a wholesale scale, of bastardy, perversion, impotency, pregnancy, abortion, murder, and marriage without even the slightest suggestion of compensating moral values."

On November 1, 1944, Joy advised Breen that Fox had optioned the work anyway and told him that Jeff (*sic*) Shurlock promised to work with the studio to develop the property into something that would pass the Code. The next day, Breen took the unusual step of writing to the file that he had spoken with Colonel Joy but did not want to send him a written response for fear that one day it might leak to the newspapers.

While this was going on, Kathleen Winsor spoke out publicly against the Hays Office, calling their censorship "absurd"[3] and defending the integrity of her work. Meanwhile, a rush of politicians, community leaders, and social clubs wrote Breen and Hays damning the book and any movie that might be made from it.

On October 9, 1945, Darryl F. Zanuck—who had returned from the war and forced William Goetz from the company—sent a copy of Philip Dunne's screenplay to Breen with assurances that "I have the impression that after you have read *Forever Amber* you will share my opinion that this screenplay has preserved a great deal of the spirit of the original and yet has managed to avoid distasteful or censorable elements." On

November 21, 1945, Breen responded to Joy with a meticulous four-page letter congratulating Fox for their work so far but pointing out dozens of changes that still needed to be made.

The exchanges continued for the next two years to the end of 1947 until the Code was satisfied. Even after that, when the film was in release, Spyros Skouras, the president of Fox, issued instructions to the company's local branches on how to physically cut the prints in order to appease Cardinal Spellman and the Catholic Legion of Decency.

What is remarkable about the Fox–Code epistolary is the efficiency with which the Breen Office read and responded to each iteration of the script, costume tests, lyrics for songs to be sung in the picture, and meetings both by phone and in person. None of these involved Preminger, but he most certainly would have been aware of the machinations as he wrapped production on *Laura* and directed *A Royal Scandal, Fallen Angel*, and *Centennial Summer* before being handed *Forever Amber*.

After all of this (and it deserves a separate book or at least a paper), *Forever Amber* was received first with skepticism and then with wide praise by critics and audiences. Although the huge production cost kept it from turning a large profit at $5 million in rentals,[4] the fact that it was made at all is something of a triumph.

As covered earlier, Otto Preminger's personal battles with the Code began in 1953 with *The Moon Is Blue*. In 1956, he decided to film *Saint Joan* from a screenplay by Graham Greene based on George Bernard Shaw's 1923 play about Joan of Arc, her trial, and her passion. What Preminger may not have known is that the Production Code Administration had been dealing with the Maid of Orleans since 1935.

In Shaw's play, which debuted three years after Joan's canonization, he presents the story of Joan of Arc and her trial by the Church for heresy in 1431. While it is now easy to criticize those who prosecuted a young woman who may very well have been schizophrenic when she heard voices of the saints commanding her into battle, Shaw took pains to specify that her inquisitors were doing what they thought was correct at the time even if hindsight has shown otherwise.

In a letter of July 18, 1935, Will Hays wrote Joseph Schenck, president of the newly formed Twentieth Century-Fox, which was considering filming the play, that it was unacceptable under the Code because it was surely to give offense to Catholics. In addition to the (factually accurate) portrayal of the Church inquisitors, Shaw's writing treats them as satiric, ironic, and/or brutal. These sentiments were echoed by Father Devlin of the Legion of Decency.

While the movie moguls were debating whether to film *Saint Joan*, a revival of the play opened at New York's Martin Beck Theatre on March 9, 1936. The cast included Katharine Cornell as Joan supported by Brian Aherne, Maurice Evans, George Coulouris, Eduardo Cianelli, John Cromwell, and Tyrone Power Jr. under Guthrie McClintic's staging. The reviews of this prestige production were forwarded to the Code Office, which remained unmoved.

Shaw was still a hot property on April 14, 1941, when British producer Gabriel Pascal sent his *Saint Joan* script to the Code Office as a precursor to turning it into a film. Pascal had scored a major hit in 1938 when he produced Shaw's *Pygmalion* starring Leslie Howard and Wendy Hiller with a screenplay by Shaw himself that won the Academy Award.[5] He had then gone on to produce the film of Shaw's *Major Barbara* in 1941 and was primed to move forward with *Saint Joan*. The Code's F. S. Harmon met with Pascal on April 14, 1941, and suggested that he retain a clerical adviser, sending a memo to Breen to that effect afterward.

On April 14, another Code employee, T. A. Lynch, submitted another assessment in which he specified that he was analyzing the play alone and not Shaw's explanatory foreword that exculpated the clergy.

Now enter Wolfgang Reinhardt, producer/screenwriter and son of German producer Max Reinhardt (a mentor of Otto Preminger). On March 11, 1943, Breen advised Reinhardt of the same reservations regarding *Saint Joan* that he had given previous producers. The Production Code Administration files are not specific, but it appears that Pascal and Reinhardt were trying to set up *Saint Joan* with David O. Selznick (or at least with Daniel O'Shea at Selznick International Pictures).

Next on Joan's dance card was Harry Cohn of Columbia Pictures. On April 23, 1943, Cohn indicated his interest but only if he could persuade Mr. Shaw to accept the changes that would be necessary to film his play to get a Code seal. Nothing further is found in the files from Cohn, but Pascal continues his presence until a hopeful letter of June 15, 1943, to Joe Breen, which Breen answered as a friend on July 14, apologizing, without saying it in so many words, that the reason he has had to oppose the play is not personal but a matter of the Code.

Nothing further is to be found from Pascal. Instead, thirteen years later, Mary Cook, Otto Preminger's secretary, sent two copies of Graham Greene's screenplay to Geoffrey Shurlock on October 23, 1956, indicating Preminger's interest. On October 30, Shurlock dutifully wrote back with two pages of "Don'ts and Be Carefuls" centering around offending the Church and actions that may be sexually suggestive.

Preminger proceeded to film *Saint Joan* after a highly publicized search for a young woman to star in it, eventually settling on eighteen-year-old Jean Seberg. Filming began in early January 1957 and rushed to completion in order to make a premiere sixteen weeks hence.

Code members Shurlock, Murphy, Vizzard, and Hodenfield screened and evaluated the finished film and gave it a Code seal on May 24, but by then, the film had already been playing for two weeks, having been released on May 8. Whether Preminger was serious or just going through the motions with the Code Administration is open for debate.

As late as 1966—the same year Jack Valenti was settling into his new office at the MPAA—Preminger was still jousting with Breen's successor, Geoffrey Shurlock. The cause this time was *Hurry Sundown*. Based on a steamy two-volume 1964 potboiler by K. B. Gilden (the married team of Katya Alpert and Bert Gilden) about a conniving white couple (Jane Fonda and Michael Caine) in the South who try to cheat African American property owners (Robert Hooks and Diahann Carroll) in a land deal, its provocative content was a perfect fit for the filmmaker's publicity-minded wheelhouse.[6] In a May 26, 1966, letter, Shurlock commended Preminger on his script (written by Horton Foote and Thomas C. Ryan) while warning him in a May 26, 1966, letter of several things that were unacceptable under the Code:

- The expletive "hell" while not basically objectionable appears quite a number of times" Pages 8, 10, 11, 62, 104, 106, 121 (twice), 143, 148, 188, 208 and 210. We suggest the advisability of omitting some of these.
- The expression "nigger" appears quite a number of times: Page 24, 35 (twice), 73, 74, 75, 107, 117 (twice), 148 (twice), and 157.
- Page 192: We could not approve the expression "god-damned." The same applies to the expression "Goddammit" on Page 198.
- Pages 55 and 80: We urge care with these scenes between Julie and Henty on the bed.

Preminger shot his film anyway and submitted it to the Production Code Administration for a Code seal. On October 31, Shurlock wrote to file of a conversation he had with Preminger in which the filmmaker refused to delete or change the following:

- Jane Fonda's suggestive licking of sax mouthpiece
- Jane Fonda on top of Michael Caine
- Michael Caine writing on top of Jane Fonda
- Michael Caine grasping Jane Fonda's breast
- Young boy to his father: "God damn nigger lover"

At loggerheads with Shurlock, Preminger appealed to Jack Valenti and Louis Nizer, the famed First Amendment trial attorney (who was partners with Arthur Krim and Robert Benjamin in United Artists; *Hurry Sundown* was a Paramount picture). On December 16, Preminger wrote to Shurlock that the situations that bothered him are not as sexy as those in the current film *A Funny Thing Happened on the Way to the Forum*.[7] "Isn't the basic idea of the new Code and its classification for mature audiences to look at the overall picture and motivations like the industry censor in England does rather than to pick on details?" Furthermore, he added, the Fonda–Caine changes would involve expensive retakes.

The conflict ended with a whimper. Preminger accepted the Code's designation of *Hurry Sundown* as SMA[8] (Suggested for Mature Audiences), which carried no age restriction, and on January 17, 1967, the film was awarded a Code seal. It was released to theatres on February 7, 1967. Receiving highly negative reviews, it returned rentals of $4,050,000 to barely break even.[9]

8

OTTO PREMINGER'S EXODUS

In 1962, just before the release of *Exodus*, his epic drama of the founding of Israel, Otto Preminger was in a meeting with the advertising and publicity department of United Artists. They were trying to decide how to present the director's possessive credit. His insistence on the billing "Otto Preminger's *Exodus*" caused one studio publicist to wisecrack, right before he was fired, "But Otto, that's what people have been wanting for years."

Otto Preminger's actual exodus was no laughing matter. Buoyed by the financial success of *Anatomy of a Murder* and *Exodus*, Preminger made a deal with Columbia to direct *The Cardinal*, an explosive drama of a priest who survives Nazis, the Ku Klux Klan, and his own demons to rise in the church. On the strength of these hits, George Weltner, the president of Paramount Pictures, signed a multipicture deal with Preminger, something that Martin Rackin, who was Paramount's combative head of production, vehemently opposed. "And then Weltner did the unforgiveable," Rackin told interviewer Walter Wagner. "He made a deal with Otto Preminger, who I regard as walking clap, the only man whose picture should be in every post office in the United States. With the lousy pictures he's made he's stolen more money from the movie business than Jesse James stole from the railroads. Jessie James was a fucking philanthropist compared to Preminger. And Weltner, in his hysteria, signed Preminger, who is not a producer, a director, or anything, He's a Viennese fucking lawyer." With one exception, the films Preminger produced under the Paramount deal bore out Rackin's morbid prediction.[1]

"Otto was like Dr. Jekyll and Mr. Hyde," says Yoram Ben-Ami, who, as a young Israeli production manager, talked his way onto Preminger's production of *Rosebud* (1975) while it was location shooting in Israel in 1974. "He couldn't concentrate. A little bit of noise made him crazy. One day we were shooting and somebody was talking while he was rehearsing the actors. He turned around to where the sound came from and pointed at somebody and said, 'You're fired!' It was a nurse. I went to her and said, 'Why did you talk?' and she said, 'I didn't say anything' and started crying. I went to Otto and said, 'Mr. Preminger, she didn't speak' and he said, 'Yes she did! Yes she did!' Then I said to him, 'If she goes, all the Israeli crew will walk away.' Pause. 'Okay, but tell her not speak again.' He always had to be right."

Ben-Ami's turn to get fired (Preminger would ultimately sack twenty people during the shoot) happened when he dared correct the director, who had staged a scene where Israeli commandos shoot a group of terrorists in the back. When the young man said that Israeli commandos would never do that, Preminger fired him. "Then while I was waiting in the car to go back to the hotel where the crew was staying, he sent a receptionist or somebody to tell me to meet Preminger at his suite. He was all sweetness, offered me a drink, and said, 'You're right. I shouldn't have the heroes in my movie shooting somebody in the back.' Then he told me to get a room next to his in the hotel." Just like that, Ben-Ami became the director's adviser on Israeli sensibilities.

Despite being taken under Preminger's wing, Ben-Ami notes, "He never took the blame on himself. He was always right and probably one of the biggest egomaniacs I ever knew. But he could also be really human," flying Ben-Ami and his wife Ani to the film's London premiere. The tutelage worked; Ben-Ami later came to America, where he produced such hit films as *Lone Wolf McQuade*, *The Lion of Africa*, and *Jury Duty*.

Film historian/critic Deac Rossell worked with Preminger in his later years during *Tell Me That You Love Me, Junie Moon*. It was quite an adventure. "He was very, very smart," Rossell appraises, "and quickly became restless. I spent several days sitting in his office alone, listening to all of his phone calls and watching all of his meetings—at this time I just did not know that this was a habit in Hollywood for young apprentices and I thought the opportunity was something unique and special. Between phone calls and meetings, which actually were few, I asked him about a lot of his early activities, and particularly about his work with fellow immigrants: the Thimig family, [Billy] Wilder, and lots of other minor characters that he cast across the background of his early films. When I say a man of principle, this was another one: he actively supported those seeking refuge from the Third Reich and from dictatorship. I was just glad to learn from him, and to see Hollywood operating: it was 1969, I was on the lot at Paramount, I was something like 23, and it was all fascinating to me. Then one day his Executive Assistant Nat Rudich took me aside and thanked me for keeping Otto busy: 'If you were not asking him questions, he would be driving us all crazy here,' he said. 'We have a lot to do in this week, and he would be so restless and so interventionist that we wouldn't get anything done.' Who knew? I was just lapping it all up. Didn't think there was anything in it at all.

"The reason that we were suddenly in Los Angeles," said Rossell, whose career took him to the Directors Guild and the British Film Institute, "was because of Otto's principles. We had been shooting for several weeks on Cape Ann, Massachusetts, where the disfigured trio of characters [in *Junie Moon*] had set up housekeeping. Then we moved to Florida to do the final week, and Otto found himself in a major dispute with the cameraman's union. Florida was double territory: if you had a New York cameraman, it was New York union territory. If you were working with a California crew, you had to hire New York union members, a pure case of featherbedding, since the Florida men would have nothing to do for top union salaries. I vividly remember a couple of the Florida union officials who came over to have a discussion about this, both wearing concealed handguns. As an Easterner, I had never seen this in real life before, and in 1969 it was, in fact, pretty rare. But these two gangsters wanted to make their point. Otto refused to hire the extra men and said he would close up the production and finish in California rather than give in to this extortion. Nobody had time to go to a court and sort it out there, as the union well knew. The Florida chapter didn't believe Otto. But he wasn't having it. We did one day of shooting on the Gulf coast, and Otto closed the production and flew off to Hollywood. Because of Otto's principles, he just would not be intimidated by anyone under any circumstances. And that's what he did to the Code, too."[2]

The Human Factor (1979) became Preminger's last picture, and it did not end well. Scripted by Tom Stoppard from Graham Greene's novel about a mid-level British Intelligence worker who does a favor for a South African Communist and has it blow back on him, it had money problems almost from the beginning. With the end of his lucrative Paramount deal, the filmmaker had to raise his own production money by preselling the film's rights in various territories. When one of the investors pulled out, stiffing the production crew for their salaries, Preminger began selling off his paintings, apartments, and other possessions to raise the money. Five years after the film's box office flop, the press reported that various creditors who still hadn't been paid sued Preminger's company, Sigma, and Preminger personally for £500,000.

In December 1971, Preminger had married Hope Bryce, who had been his costume coordinator since 1958, while he was married to Mary Gardner, whom he divorced in 1959. Preminger and Bryce had two children. In 1944, he had also been romantically involved with famed ecdysiast Gypsy Rose Lee and sired a son, Erik Lee, who used the name Erik Kirkland until Gypsy died in 1970, after which he publicly took his father's surname.

Preminger, trying to get another project together after *The Human Factor*, wanted to film *Open Secret*, the story of executed atomic spies Julius and Ethel Rosenberg.[3] Unable to do so, he remained a public figure doing talk shows, documentaries, and being a man-about-town. He was invariably charming, if opinionated, and made people wonder why he was known behind his back as "Otto the Ogre." By 1980, it was apparent that he was having memory lapses, which the family at first denied. He died on April 23, 1986, at age eighty of lung cancer complicated by Alzheimer's disease.

"Preminger was highly intelligent and he knew how the movie systems worked," summarizes Rossell, looking back on the man who inspired, educated, and sometimes frightened him, "so I am certain that he saw a whiff of publicity, a whiff of scandal, and a whiff of controversy in any steps that he took with abandoning the Code, with breaking the Blacklist, with upholding any number of liberal causes that were essential to so many of his films. But that whiff, that odor, that cynicism, that calculation, was only a flurry around the hard core of his principles, which were always his deeply-rooted starting point. You can't make a movie like *The Moon Is Blue* just because you want to challenge the Production Code. Too much work, too risky. You have to believe something is there that makes a good film; in this case a breezy modern-ish romantic comedy that a was more contemporary in its ethics and relationships than the rather stodgy Code. And when Joe Breen intervened in the process, Otto just wasn't having anything to do with it. And, of course, he knew that [Arthur] Krim and [Robert] Benjamin, the new United Artists execs, would agree with him, which they did."[4]

After the Motion Picture Production Code was replaced in 1968 by the letter rating system (q.v.), the MPAA made its process more inscrutable than it had been for the previous thirty-seven years. Just as what are known as "community standards" change over the years as people become more sophisticated, the Board attempts to modify their rating criteria to coincide with maturing public mores. This is something that the Hays, Breen, and Shurlock offices never did. As Kirby Dick reported in his 2006 documentary *This Film Is Not Yet Rated*, not only are the criteria seemingly written in smoke, but the identities of the people wielding them are hidden. The Production Code Administration records at the MPAA library end in 1967, so there is no way to assess what, if any, considerations were given to the films Preminger made post–*Hurry Sundown*, that is, *Skiddoo* (1968; rated R), *Tell Me That You Move Me, Junie Moon* (1970, rated PG), *Such Good Friends* (1971, rated R), *Rosebud* (1975, rated PG), and *The Human Factor* (1979, rated R).

Otto Preminger's artistic legacy as a filmmaker may be up for discussion but not his legacy as a warrior for social progress and human rights. He didn't just fight evil; he fought ignorance back in the days before the two became one.

9

JACK VALENTI AND THE RATING SYSTEM

It must be remembered that, over the nine years that the Production Code Administration under its various people was parrying with Preminger, they were also dealing with every other movie that Hollywood was making. They would comment on potential properties, story treatments, multiple drafts of screenplays, shooting scripts, rough cuts, final edits, and the advertising and publicity campaigns that went with the estimated 4,000 titles produced from 1954 to 1962.[1]

They were not run as a charity. Their expenses were borne entirely by their member film companies and the occasional independent producer who wanted a Code seal. Today, even without the Code, an MPAA rating can cost between $2,500 and $25,000 depending on a film's negative cost (budget before distribution expenses) from $500,000 to $75 million. Modern mega-budget productions do not presently appear on the MPAA's website. Short subjects and reissues are $2,500. One does not have to be an MPAA member for the Classification and Rating Administration (CARA) to assess a rating.[2]

By the mid-1960s, the Code was feeling pressure to catch up with changes in the social fabric of America. The first move in that direction came at the hands of fate on August 22, 1963, when MPAA President

Eric Johnston died following a series of strokes. His post went unfilled for three years until September 1966, when Jack Valenti was hired.

Jack Joseph Valenti, born in Houston, Texas, in 1921, went from advertising to lobbying to a position in the Lyndon Baines Johnson White House as speechwriter and special adviser to the president. If it sounds like a purposely vague post, that's what it was meant to be, as both Valenti and Johnson were past masters at arm-twisting and backroom dealing, both of which were lubricated with Texas charm. Given leave in 1966 to take over the leaderless MPAA, Valenti discovered that he had inherited an organization that was running on fumes and was desperate to modernize itself lest it be put out of business. Many filmmakers were already pounding at the gates of maturity: Arthur Penn with *Bonnie and Clyde*, Mike Nichols with *Who's Afraid of Virginia Woolf?*, Richard Lester with *Petulia*, John Huston with *Reflections in a Golden Eye*, Cornel Wilde with *Beach Red*, Mark Rydell with *The Fox*, and Richard Brooks with *In Cold Blood*, among others, and even Otto Preminger's otherwise unremarkable *Hurry Sundown*. Some were released with the stopgap designation "SMA: Suggested for Mature Audiences," used from 1966 to mid-1967.

Taking charge, Valenti, in consultation with his Board, community leaders, and parents' groups, created what became known as the Movie Ratings. Where, hitherto, there were specific rules, the letter ratings were more nebulous by design so as to reflect changing community standards. In effect, Valenti put one genie back in the bottle and released another one. For more than fifty years, nobody has been able to figure out definitively what changes a G into a PG, a PG into an R, or anything in between. The membership of CARA is secret, and its deliberations are never made public, only the verdicts. Filmmaker

Kirby Dick came closest to cracking both the code and the Code in his 2006 documentary *This Film Is Not Yet Rated* (written by himself, Eddie Schmidt, and Matt Patterson), appropriately raising the ire of the MPAA. After CARA gave the film an NC-17, Dick and IFC Films decided, unsurprisingly, to release it without a rating.

When the MPAA announced their original letter ratings on November 1, 1968, they registered their G, M, and R as trademarks but purposely did not register the X because they wanted producers to be able to self-apply it. This quickly led to its being appropriated by the porn industry. When the MPAA introduced the NC-17 rating in September 1990, they were more diligent in protecting it.

In early 1969, just after he announced his revised Code, MPAA President Jack Valenti embarked on a tour of major colleges to explain it to student leaders and the media. This was his acknowledgment that the youth audience had become the prime moviegoing demographic as well as the determining factor in what new films were being produced. It was a bold move, but Valenti was no stranger to boldness; after all, his duties to President Johnson had included defending LBJ's waging of the Vietnam War.

At the time, old-line Hollywood was adrift. The founding moguls had no clue what young moviegoing audiences wanted to see. By 1968, the studio bosses who hadn't died or retired had begun selling their fiefdoms to insurance companies, parking lot owners, oil magnates, and talent agencies. The inheriting bean counters turned to the growing number of young filmmakers who were being disgorged from an increasing number of film schools. They had become Hollywood's—and thus Valenti's—target audience.

As it happened, I (hereinafter "Author") was one of a small group of what were called "student leaders" invited to a February 11, 1969, confab at Boston University's George Sherman Union, and I tape-recorded Valenti's colloquy. He had come to Boston University with director Noel Black to show Black's extraordinary new film *Pretty Poison*. This transcript of that exchange, edited only for clarity, is the first time it has appeared anywhere:

Jack Valenti: The rating system was brought in because it's been my judgment—and I'm gonna take credit for its success and am, unhappily, the one on whose shoulders will fall all the blame if it fails—had to come into being because of a changing society. Mores and customs changed and the movies are different than they were a generation ago, just as society is different. But to say "different" is not to say "wrong" or to say "misshapen." We're trying out the rating system to make it possible for a young filmmaker or an older filmmaker to have freedom to express themselves, freedom to choose a subject, and freedom in the way he chooses to tell it. What we're doing is rating films for children because we believe that until a child is old enough or mature enough to assess a value, he may not understand, or may be persuaded by wrong values because of immaturity, in the picture. We think an adult should be able to choose any picture he wants to see, but we think that there's a difference with children. We rate films according to the acceptability of the film as it pertains to children under sixteen.[3]

When you read about censorship you realize how ludicrous it is and how it's lunacy for one man to pass a judgment on his peers. It's imperfect, but all we're doing is rating films so that parents instantly know the content of a movie. This doesn't mean that it's a good movie or a bad movie. It doesn't mean it's gonna be box office or not. It does mean that when you see a G it means it's good for all ages. There's nothing embarrassing in it. Now, while a *Lion in Winter* might be a G, so might a Walt Disney picture but, where a young child may not understand a *Lion in Winter*, we don't think there's anything in there that's embarrassing. With M we're saying that there might be something that might be embarrassing or might be objectionable; we don't know, we suggest you find out more about it. Meanwhile, we're not restricting anybody, we're just labeling. R is an adult film. No question about it. There's something in there that's either violence or language or sex that we think a young child of sixteen ought not to be there without his parent or an adult guardian to explain it to him. X would be a patently adult film and someone under sixteen just ought not see it.

Author: There's a new film from Paramount called *If . . .* by Lindsay Anderson that has been given an X rating. It's about campus unrest and ends in violence. The review in the *Boston Herald* said that it could be a teaching film for adults and a broadening film for young people.

Valenti: That comes under a judgment. I have not seen *If . . .* , so I can't make a personal judgment. You have seven people in California who are neither gods nor fools. They are all in the business of monitoring and appraising films. They make a judgment but you understand that the judgment is not based on what an educated young man like yourself thinks about it. You've got to set yourself down and think about it in another milieu, that is to say, as a parent. If I went in to see this film, how would I feel about having my ten-year-old daughter or nine-year-old son with me? That's the thing you want to think about. Now, to me, the freest, wildest left-wing liberals in the world wouldn't quarrel with that because freedom of expression is obviously embedded in the whole ethos of the American spirit. But a child is not quite ready. That's how we judge a new film. So when you see the ratings, it's not on intellectual content or lack of intellectual content. It's based on common sense. It's based on common sense, a kind of gut-level instinctual feeling of how parents would feel about that particular film. There's nothing to prevent you from taking a child to see an R. Now, an X film, there is some contention there. I was personally opposed to an X category myself. I didn't want to go any higher than R. But you find, if you want to move things along, you have to reshape or reform some of your own views so you can get someone else to agree with you. So in order to get this system through, the X had to be part of it.

Author: You said before [in his earlier opening remarks] that there is a correlation between educational level and filmgoing. Wouldn't the X rating defeat the purpose of allowing people who are intellectually able to understand an X film from seeing it?

Valenti: Are you saying a thirteen- or fourteen-year-old?

Author: If their parents say yes, why not?

Valenti: Well, what you're talking about is 3 to 8 percent of movies. So far only 5 percent of movies have been rated X.[4] But that leaves 95 percent of films made, 28 percent of which are R films which a parent can take his child to see. I don't find the X films a significant number, either quality or amount, for me to worry about at this time. Could change; next year we might have nothing but X films. Then we'd have to look at our hole card. I don't know. But at this point it's not significant. [The ratings] are not censorship for this reason: we don't ban a film. We don't cut a scene. Nobody cuts anything unless [the filmmaker] agrees to it. Well, you may say that's commercial censorship. Remember this: the director or a crew have rights, but the investors have rights too. The liberty of one man ends where the rights of another man begin. The investor can tell a filmmaker, "You make this film any way you want it, but I must have an R rating or an M or a G or I can't sell it." Neither civil nor canon law says he has to accept that contract but, if he agrees, he must abide by that contract. For many years there was a boilerplate in every contract that said "this picture must receive a Code seal" that's been there for years. If you sign the contract, you have to abide by it.

Author: Would you deny that the ratings are a façade to avoid federal censorship?

Valenti: I wouldn't deny that at all; that's one of the reasons for it. We're fighting federal censorship with all the fervor we can summon. I think it's wrong. It is philosophically, morally wrong and, most of all it, is as pragmatically wrong as it is constitutionally wrong. The rating system is a weapon to show that this industry can do for itself what an enterprise or a family or a business or a group or an organization rather than the government can intrude with the bludgeon of the law. The rating system is the greatest shield of freedom that a filmmaker could ever have, that a critic could ever want. Because if you pass a law [to] judge a film [on] a political bias, then you are embarking on the slipperyest and most torturous path a society can take, in my judgment, because not only is it going to constrain and constrict him in every way, but where do you draw the line?

Valenti warned that there were bills poised in legislatures in many localities by people opposed to views "contrary to their own." He asked how "any rational person" could object to the rating system. This being a college audience, some people did, insisting that self-censorship instills hesitation out of fear of conflict. Valenti disagreed.

Valenti: You can make anything and put it on the screen as long as it doesn't collide with criminal obscenity law. What's wrong with that? With the exception of one exhibitor[5] of the seventy-five or so leading chain operators, all the exhibitors agree to it. I'd say that 98 percent of the creative community in this land would accept that. That in itself is a kind of miracle. Who can tell if we're going to need a rating system five or ten years from now? I just think that it is in the interest of a free, unfettered industry that we always mind the society in which we live. Five years may see this country change so radically that who knows? My own opinion is that the pendulum will swing the other way and that people will object to a four-letter obscenity to express a thought. That it shows a guy with no talent. You want to show love without copulation. Anger without obscenity. That takes talent.

Implicit in Valenti's remarks about parental guidance was that, in advising parents of film contents, the MPAA was also advising exhibitors of films that might run afoul of community standards and bring about legal sanction. Because of this, some exhibitors would choose to ignore or self-apply the ratings on certain films that drew public scrutiny. *The Exorcist* may have been rated R by the MPAA but, in some communities, it was treated at the box office like an X. Conversely, *The Panic in Needle Park*, rated R for showing drug use (shades of *The Man with the Golden Arm*), was thrown open to unaccompanied minors in some cities because of its powerful anti-drug message. This was wildcatting by exhibitors who knew their community standards. The cogent point is that the Hays Code, formed in fear and caution, would have tied filmmakers' hands in perpetuity had it not been challenged by adventurous writers and directors over the course of many decades and then assaulted head-on by Otto Preminger at the exact moment when it was most vulnerable.

After he had seen Hollywood begin to function with relative freedom under his rating system, Jack Valenti summarized his work with typical Texas humor, telling a reporter in the summer of 1969, "When I invented this system, which is totally voluntary, it was not to placate critics—it was to protect parents. I haven't heard from a single parent who said, 'Gee, I wish you'd kept that orgy in there.' I think this system is doing exactly what it was intended to do."

Valenti retired from the MPAA in 2004 and became founding president of Friends of the Global Fight Against AIDS, Tuberculosis, and Malaria. He died from a stroke on April 26, 2007.

It might be cynical (but not inaccurate) to insist that while the Production Code has changed over its 100-year history, its purpose has not.

In the beginning, as now, its stated mission is to protect the public from objectionable material on the screen. Behind that promise, however, is its unstated mission, which is to prevent the public from having the government establish its own censorship system. Whatever moral impetus led When Will Hays, Joseph Breen, Geoffrey Shurlock, Eric Johnson, and Jack Valenti to introduce their codes, the pragmatic reason was to keep the government's hands out Hollywood's business.

This is because the MPAA is fundamentally a trade organization, a legislative lobbyist for its member companies. Its goals are commerce first, artistic freedom second. Their mission, other than CARA, is stopping piracy, fighting foreign tariffs on American films, freeing blocked studio income trapped in international economies, reducing runaway production, and backing tax incentives that promote domestic film production. During his reign, Jack Valenti faced these challenges with the finesse that made him LBJ's confidant. Among his greatest battles was a fight over "blind bidding," a practice by which exhibitors were compelled to place competitive bids for new films without being able to see them first. Studios justified this by saying that they were finishing their movies so close to release dates that screenings were impractical, a facile excuse at best. But these matters, while crucial to the industry, are esoteric at best to the general public. It was—and remains—the issue of censorship versus screen freedom that inspired, maintained, and still dominates the activities of the MPAA. Morals may have changed over the past 100 years, but the threat to freedom has the same single-minded goal. Anybody who thinks "it's only a movie" is missing the point.

APPENDIX A
PRODUCTION CODE ADMINISTRATION EVALUATION FORM FOR
ANATOMY OF A MURDER

Employees of the Production Code Administration, in addition to making notes about objectionable lines or scenes in scripts headed for production, completed a written "Analysis of Film Content" for each finished film submitted for a Code seal. This form is an attempt to make a subjective process appear objective. The four-page evaluation for *Anatomy of a Murder* is being shown because the film it analyzes has more characters and complex situations than *The Moon Is Blue*.

Abbreviations

PROM = prominent

MIN = minimal

INCI-D'T'L = incidental

STR = straight

COM = comic

S&C = straight and comic

SYM = sympathetic

UN-SYM = unsympathetic

S&U = sympathetic and unsympathetic

IN-DIF = indifferent

DIS-HON = dishonest in their portrayal

FOR = foreign

NOT CLEAR = not clear

ANALYSIS OF FILM CONTENT

PART ONE - GENERAL

COPY FOR:	
NEW YORK:	HOLLYWOOD:
RESEARCH...... [ ]	P.C.A. FILES.. [✓]
FILES......... [ ]	RESEARCH...... [ ]
MPEA.......... [ ]	
.... [ ]	.... [ ]

COLUMN		COLUMN	
1-4	TITLE: **ANATOMY OF A MURDER**	32,33	PERIOD: **Contemporary**
5-10	P.C.A. APPROVAL DATE: **6/18/59**		MAJOR LOCALES (A): **Iron City, Michigan**
11-15	P.C.A. SEAL NUMBER: **19294**		
16-19	FOOTAGE: **14,534**	34-36	

MAJOR LOCALES (B):

20,21	TYPE: **Drama-Courtroom**	CITY........ [ ]1	RURAL.......... [ ]4
22	FEATURE [x]1 SHORT [ ]2	SUBURBAN.... [ ]2	UNDEVELOPED AREAS [ ]5
23	DOMESTIC [x]1 FOREIGN [ ]2	SMALL TOWN.. [x]3 NOT CLEAR....... [ ]6
24	B. & W. [x]1 COLOR [ ]2 TONED [ ]3	OTHER: _____ [ ]7

37

SETTINGS (A): **Street Scenes-Bars-Home-County Courthouse-Lunch Stand-Country Inn-Jail-Beauty Parlor-Trailer Park-RR Station-Highways-Hospital-Convertible**

55-57	PRODUCER (CO.): **Carlyle Prodns., Inc.**
	PRODUCER (INDIV.): **Otto Preminger**
	DIRECTOR: _____ " " _____
	SCREEN WRITER: **Wendell Mayes**
25,26	WHERE FILMED: **Michigan**
27,28	DISTRIBUTOR: **Columbia**

SETTINGS (B):

VERY WEALTHY.. [ ]1	MODERATE..... [x]3
WELL-TO-DO.... [ ]2	POOR......... [ ]4
	NOT CLEAR.... [ ]5

MATERIAL SOURCE:

BIOGRAPHY...................... [ ]1	38	
COMIC STRIP.................... [ ]2		FOREIGN LANGUAGE(S) IN ADDITION TO ENGLISH: **None**
FOLKLORE....................... [ ]3		
NOVEL **by Robert Traver**...... [x]4	39,40	FOREIGN COUNTRIES TREATED:
ORIGINAL SCREEN STORY.......... [ ]5		
RADIO PROGRAM.................. [ ]6		
SHORT STORY.................... [ ]7		
STAGE PLAY..................... [ ]8		
OTHER: _____ [ ]9	41	

	SYM.	UNSYM.	S.&U.	INDIF.
42				
43 CANADA.....	[ ]1	[ ]2	[ ]3	[ ]4
44 CHINA......	[ ]1	[ ]2	[ ]3	[ ]4
ENGLAND....	[ ]1	[ ]2	[ ]3	[ ]4
FRANCE.....	[ ]1	[ ]2	[ ]3	[ ]4

SIGNIFICANT STORY ELEMENTS (ANGLES):

FOREIGN...... [ ]1	POLITICAL.... [ ]7	44	GERMANY.... [ ]1 [ ]2 [ ]3 [ ]4
HISTORICAL... [ ]2	PSYCHOLOGICAL [ ]8	45	ITALY...... [ ]1 [ ]2 [ ]3 [ ]4
JUVENILE..... [ ]3	RACIAL....... [ ]9	46	JAPAN...... [ ]1 [ ]2 [ ]3 [ ]4
MEDICAL...... [ ]4	RELIGIOUS.... [ ]0	47	MEXICO..... [ ]1 [ ]2 [ ]3 [ ]4
MILITARY..... [ ]5	SCIENTIFIC... [ ]V	48	RUSSIA..... [ ]1 [ ]2 [ ]3 [ ]4
EDUCATIONAL.. [ ]6	FAMILY LIFE.. [x]X	49	OTHERS: _____

30		

ENDING:

30	HAPPY [x]1 UNHAPPY [ ]2 MORAL [ ]3	
31	OTHER: _____ [ ]4	50,51

QT. 76	YR. 77-8	CARD 01	PAGE 1

APPENDIX A

PART TWO - PORTRAYAL OF PROFESSIONS

TITLE: ANATOMY OF A MURDER

PROFESSION	ROLE (1) PROM	(2) MIN	(3) INCI-D'T'L	CHAR. (a) STR	(5) COM	(6) S&C	(7) SYM	(8) UN-SYM	(9) S&U	(0) IN-DIF	(v) DIS-HON*	(x) FOR**
Lawyers:												
James Stewart	X			X			X					
Arthur O'Connell	X			X			X					
District Attorneys:												
Prosecuting Attorney Brooks West	X			X			X					
Ass't Atty. Gen. George C. Scott	X			X			X					
Judge Joseph N. Welch	X			X			X					
U.S. Military (Army):												
Lt. Ben Gazzara	X			X					X			
Group			X							X		
Sheriff			X	X			X					
Dep. Sheriff			X	X			X					
" " , gp.			X	X					X			
Police Detective			X	X				X				
Coroner			X	X				X				
Doctor, gp. of 3			X	X				X				
" #4			X	X				X			X	

* Check this column if professional character is *inefficient or dishonest* in the performance of his professional duties.

** Check this column if character is *both* of foreign birth and, in all probability, not a citizen of the United States.

PART THREE - PORTRAYAL OF "RACES" AND NATIONALS

"RACE" OR NATIONAL	ROLE (1) PROM	(2) MIN	(3) INCI-D'T'L	CHAR. (4) STR	(5) COM	(6) S&C	(7) SYM	(8) UN-SYM	(9) S&U	(0) IN-DIF	U.S. CITIZEN (v) YES	(x) NO	(-) NOT CLEAR
Canadian:													
Girl Hotel Manager		X		X			X					X	
Negro:													
Dance Band Group			X	X						X	X		
Train Porter			X	X						X	X		

APPENDIX A

PART FOUR - LIQUOR (CARD 05)

COLUMN

1-4   TITLE:_____ANATOMY OF A MURDER_____

5   Treatment of Liquor: None shown or consumed ( )1 Shown only ( )2 Consumed (x)3

6   If Liquor consumed, amount of drinking: Very Little ( )1 Moderately (x)2 Much ( )3

Where Liquor consumed:

Cafe, Restaurant	( )1	Dwelling Place	(x)1
Saloon, Bar	(x)2	Office or Business Place	( )2
Night Club	( )3	Other	( )3

7

8   What does character(s) drink: Wine ( )1 Beer (x)2 Hard liquor (x)3 Unidentified ( )4

9   Is actual drunkenness portrayed: Yes ( )1 No (x)2

QT. ___ YR. ___   CARD 05
76   77-78

PART FIVE - CRIME (CARD 06)

1-4   (Title Code)

5   Does picture depict crime? Yes (x)1 No ( )2 Important story point (x)3
Incidental ( )4

6 7   Describe crimes depicted: **Rape and Murder before opening scene**

8 9

Does story tend to enlist the sympathy of the audience for the criminal(s)?
10   Yes ( )1 No ( )2 Both Yes and No (x)3

11   Fate of Criminals:

Killed (x)1
Death by accident ( )2
Punished by law ( )3
Suicide ( )4
Reform ( )5
Mental Suffering ( )6
Other (x)7   **Exonerated**
No punishment ( )8

QT. ___ YR. ___   CARD 06
76   77-78

Page 3.

APPENDIX A

PART SIX - SOCIOLOGICAL FACTORS

COL. CODE

1-4 _____ TITLE:_____ <u>ANATOMY OF A MURDER</u>_____

5 _____ Is violence depicted: Yes ( )1 No (x)2
               If so, in which form: Shooting ( )1 Knifing ( )2 Sword play ( )3 Strangling ( )4
                                       Torture ( )5 Punch ( )6 Fist fight ( )7 Flogging ( )8
                                       War ( )9 Other ( )0

6 _____ Remarks:_____

7 _____ Is gambling depicted: Yes ( )1 No (x)2 Important story point ( )3 Incidental ( )4
        If depicted, describe:_____

8 _____ Is courtroom depicted: Yes (x)1 No ( )2 Dignified (x)3 Otherwise ( )4
        If depicted, describe: <u>**Trial on murder charge**</u>_____

9 _____ Are prayers said or religious ceremonies performed: Yes ( )1 No (x)2
        If so, describe:_____

10 _____ Is wedding ceremony shown in picture: Yes ( )1 No (x)2 Dignified ( )3 Otherwise ( )4
11 _____ If so, by whom is ceremony performed: Clergyman ( )1 J. of P. ( )2 Judge ( )3 Other ( )4

12 _____ Is divorce an element in the picture: Yes (x)1 No ( )2
13 _____ Does divorce occur in the picture: Yes ( )1 No (x)2
14 _____ Is divorce an important story point ( )1 Minor (x)2 Incidental ( )3
15 _____ Are characters involved important (x)1 Minor ( )2 Incidental ( )3

16 _____ Is adultery an element in the picture: Yes ( )1 No (x)2
17 _____ Does adultery occur in the picture: Yes ( )1 No ( )2
18 _____ Is adultery an important story point ( )1 Minor ( )2 Incidental ( )3
19 _____ Are characters involved important ( )1 Minor ( )2 Incidental ( )3

20 _____ Is illicit sex an element in the picture: Yes ( )1 No (x)2
21 _____ Does illicit sex occur in the picture: Yes ( )1 No ( )2
22 _____ Is illicit sex an important story point ( )1 Minor ( )2 Incidental ( )3
23 _____ Are characters involved important ( )1 Minor ( )2 Incidental ( )3

24 _____ Is illegitimacy shown (x)1 Indicated ( )2 Not shown ( )3
25 _____ Is seduction shown ( )1 Indicated ( )2 Not shown (x)3
26 _____ Is rape shown ( )1 Indicated (x)2 Not shown ( )3

QT.   YR.   CARD 07
‾‾‾   ‾‾‾‾
76   77-78

STAFF (6/16/59)

APPENDIX B
TEXT OF THE CODE

MPAA – The Motion Picture Production Code – MPPDA – October 1927
The 36 Don'ts and Be Carefuls

Published In October 1927 By the Motion Picture Producers and Distributors of America (MPPDA)

Resolved: That those things which are included in the following list shall not appear in pictures produced by the members of this Association, irrespective of the manner in which they are treated:

1. Pointed profanity—by either title or lip—this includes the words "God," "Lord," "Jesus" "Christ" (unless they be used reverently in connection with proper religious ceremonies), "hell," "damn," "Gawd," and every other profane and vulgar expression however it may be spelled;

2. Any licentious or suggestive nudity—in fact or in silhouette; and any lecherous or licentious notice thereof by other characters in the picture;

3. The illegal traffic in drugs;

4. Any inference of sex perversion;

5. White slavery;

6. Miscegenation (sex relationship between the white and black races);

7. Sex hygiene and venereal diseases;

8. Scenes of actual childbirth—in fact or in silhouette;

9. Children's sex organs;

10. Ridicule of the clergy;

11. Willful offence to any nation, race or creed;

And it be further *Resolved:* That special care be exercised in the manner in which the following subjects are treated, to the end that vulgarity and suggestiveness may be eliminated and that good taste may be emphasized:

1. The use of the flag;

2. International relations (avoiding picturizing in an unfavorable light another country's religion, history, institutions, prominent people and citizenry);

3. Arson;

4. The use of firearms;

5. Theft, robbery, safe-cracking, and dynamiting of trains, mines, buildings, etc. (having in mind the effect which a too-detailed description of these may have upon the moron);

6. Brutality and possible gruesomeness;

7. Technique of committing murder by whatever method;

8. Methods of smuggling;

9. Third-degree methods;

10. Actual hangings or electrocutions as legal punishment for crime;

11. Sympathy for criminals;

12. Attitude toward public characters and institutions;

13. Sedition;

14. Apparent cruelty to children and animals;

15. Branding of people or animals;

16. The sale of women, or of a woman selling her virtue;

17. Rape or attempted rape;

18. First-night scenes;

19. Man and woman in bed together;

20. Deliberate seduction of girls;

21. The institution of marriage;

22. Surgical operations;

23. The use of drugs;

24. Titles or scenes having to do with law enforcement or law-enforcing officers;

25. Excessive or lustful kissing, particularly when one character or the other is a "heavy"

A Code to Govern the Making of Talking, Synchronized and Silent Motion Pictures. Formulated and formally adopted by The Association of Motion Picture Producers, Inc. and The Motion Picture Producers and Distributors of America, Inc. in March 1930.

Motion picture producers recognize the high trust and confidence which have been placed in them by the people of the world and which have made motion pictures a universal form of entertainment.

They recognize their responsibility to the public because of this trust and because entertainment and art are important influences in the life of a nation.

Hence, though regarding motion pictures primarily as entertainment without any explicit purpose of teaching or propaganda, they know that the motion picture within its own field of entertainment may be directly responsible for spiritual or moral progress, for higher types of social life, and for much correct thinking.

During the rapid transition from silent to talking pictures they have realized the necessity and the opportunity of subscribing to a Code to govern the production of talking pictures and of re-acknowledging this responsibility.

On their part, they ask from the public and from public leaders a sympathetic understanding of their purposes and problems and a spirit of cooperation that will allow them the freedom and opportunity necessary to bring the motion picture to a still higher level of wholesome entertainment for all the people.

General Principles

1. No picture shall be produced that will lower the moral standards of those who see it. Hence the sympathy of the audience should never be thrown to the side of crime, wrongdoing, evil or sin.
2. Correct standards of life, subject only to the requirements of drama and entertainment, shall be presented.
3. Law, natural or human, shall not be ridiculed, nor shall sympathy be created for its violation.

Particular Applications

I. Crimes Against the Law. These shall never be presented in such a way as to throw sympathy with the crime as against law and justice or to inspire others with a desire for imitation.

1. Murder
   a. The technique of murder must be presented in a way that will not inspire imitation.
   b. Brutal killings are not to be presented in detail.
   c. Revenge in modern times shall not be justified.
2. Methods of Crime should not be explicitly presented.
   a. Theft, robbery, safe-cracking, and dynamiting of trains, mines, buildings, etc., should not be detailed in method.
   b. Arson must subject to the same safeguards.
   c. The use of firearms should be restricted to the essentials.
   d. Methods of smuggling should not be presented.
3. Illegal drug traffic must never be presented.
4. The use of liquor in American life, when not required by the plot or for proper characterization, will not be shown.

II. Sex: The sanctity of the institution of marriage and the home shall be upheld. Pictures shall not infer that low forms of sex relationship are the accepted or common thing.

1. Adultery, sometimes necessary plot material, must not be explicitly treated, or justified, or presented attractively.
2. Scenes of Passion
   a. They should not be introduced when not essential to the plot.

    b. Excessive and lustful kissing, lustful embraces, suggestive postures and gestures, are not to be shown.

    c. In general passion should so be treated that these scenes do not stimulate the lower and baser element.

3. Seduction or Rape

    a. They should never be more than suggested, and only when essential for the plot, and even then never shown by explicit method.

    b. They are never the proper subject for comedy.

4. Sex perversion or any inference to it is forbidden.

5. White slavery shall not be treated.

6. Miscegenation (sex relationships between the white and black races) is forbidden.

7. Sex hygiene and venereal diseases are not subjects for motion pictures.

8. Scenes of actual child birth, in fact or in silhouette, are never to be presented.

9. Children's sex organs are never to be exposed.

III. Vulgarity: The treatment of low, disgusting, unpleasant, though not necessarily evil, subjects should always be subject to the dictates of good taste and a regard for the sensibilities of the audience.

IV. Obscenity: Obscenity in word, gesture, reference, song, joke, or by suggestion (even when likely to be understood only by part of the audience) is forbidden.

V. Profanity: Pointed profanity (this includes the words, God, Lord, Jesus, Christ—unless used reverently—Hell, S.O.B., damn, Gawd), or every other profane or vulgar expression however used, is forbidden.

VI. Costume:

1. Complete nudity is never permitted. This includes nudity in fact or in silhouette, or any lecherous or licentious notice thereof by other characters in the picture.
2. Undressing scenes should be avoided, and never used save where essential to the plot.
3. Indecent or undue exposure is forbidden.
4. Dancing or costumes intended to permit undue exposure or indecent movements in the dance are forbidden.

VII. Dances

1. Dances suggesting or representing sexual actions or indecent passions are forbidden.
2. Dances which emphasize indecent movements are to be regarded as obscene.

VIII. Religion

1. No film or episode may throw ridicule on any religious faith.
2. Ministers of religion in their character as ministers of religion should not be used as comic characters or as villains.

3. Ceremonies of any definite religion should be carefully and respectfully handled.

IX. Locations: The treatment of bedrooms must be governed by good taste and delicacy.

X. National Feelings

1. The use of the Flag shall be consistently respectful.
2. The history, institutions, prominent people and citizenry of other nations shall be represented fairly.

XI. Titles: Salacious, indecent, or obscene titles shall not be used.

XII. Repellent Subjects: The following subjects must be treated within the careful limits of good taste:

1. Actual hangings or electrocutions as legal punishments for crime.
2. Third degree methods.
3. Brutality and possible gruesomeness.
4. Branding of people or animals.
5. Apparent cruelty to children or animals.
6. The sale of women, or a woman selling her virtue.
7. Surgical operations.

Reasons Supporting the Preamble of the Code

I. Theatrical motion pictures, that is, pictures intended for the theatre as distinct from pictures intended for churches, schools, lecture halls, educational movements, social reform movements, etc., are primarily to be regarded as ENTERTAINMENT.

Mankind has always recognized the importance of entertainment and its value in rebuilding the bodies and souls of human beings.

But it has always recognized that entertainment can be a character either HELPFUL or HARMFUL to the human race, and in consequence has clearly distinguished between:

a. Entertainment which tends to improve the race, or at least to re-create and rebuild human beings exhausted with the realities of life; and

b. Entertainment which tends to degrade human beings, or to lower their standards of life and living.

Hence the MORAL IMPORTANCE of entertainment is something which has been universally recognized. It enters intimately into the lives of men and women and affects them closely; it occupies their minds and affections during leisure hours; and ultimately touches the whole of their lives. A man may be judged by his standard of entertainment as easily as by the standard of his work.

So correct entertainment raises the whole standard of a nation.

Wrong entertainment lowers the whole living conditions and moral ideals of a race.

Note, for example, the healthy reactions to healthful sports, like baseball, golf; the unhealthy reactions to sports like cockfighting, bullfighting, bear baiting, etc.

Note, too, the effect on ancient nations of gladiatorial combats, the obscene plays of Roman times, etc.

II. Motion pictures are very important as ART. Though a new art, possibly a combination art, it has the same object as the other arts, the presentation of human thought, emotion, and experience, in terms of an appeal to the soul through the senses.

Here, as in entertainment, Art enters intimately into the lives of human beings. Art can be morally good, lifting men to higher levels. This has been done through good music, great painting, authentic fiction, poetry, drama. Art can be morally evil in its effects. This is the case clearly enough with unclean art, indecent books, suggestive drama. The effect on the lives of men and women are obvious.

Note: It has often been argued that art itself is unmoral, neither good nor bad. This is true of the THING which is music, painting, poetry, etc. But the THING is the PRODUCT of some person's mind, and the intention of that mind was either good or bad morally when it produced the thing. Besides, the thing has its EFFECT upon those who come into contact with it. In both these ways, that is, as a product of a mind and as the cause of definite effects, it has a deep moral significance and unmistakable moral quality.

Hence: The motion pictures, which are the most popular of modern arts for the masses, have their moral quality from the intention of the minds which produce them and from their effects on the moral lives and reactions of their audiences. This gives them a most important morality.

1. They reproduce the morality of the men who use the pictures as a medium for the expression of their ideas and ideals.

2. They affect the moral standards of those who, through the screen, take in these ideas and ideals. In the case of motion pictures, the effect may be particularly emphasized because no art has so quick

and so widespread an appeal to the masses. It has become in an incredibly short period the art of the multitudes.

III. The motion picture, because of its importance as entertainment and because of the trust placed in it by the peoples of the world, has special MORAL OBLIGATIONS:

A. Most arts appeal to the mature. This art appeals at once to every class, mature, immature, developed, undeveloped, law abiding, criminal. Music has its grades for different classes; so has literature and drama. This art of the motion picture, combining as it does the two fundamental appeals of looking at a picture and listening to a story, at once reaches every class of society.

B. By reason of the mobility of film and the ease of picture distribution, and because the possibility of duplicating positives in large quantities, this art reaches places unpenetrated by other forms of art.

C. Because of these two facts, it is difficult to produce films intended for only certain classes of people. The exhibitors' theatres are built for the masses, for the cultivated and the rude, the mature and the immature, the self-respecting and the criminal. Films, unlike books and music, can with difficulty be confined to certain selected groups.

D. The latitude given to film material cannot, in consequence, be as wide as the latitude given to book material. In addition:

a. A book describes; a film vividly presents. One presents on a cold page; the other by apparently living people.

b. A book reaches the mind through words merely; a film reaches the eyes and ears through the reproduction of actual events.

c. The reaction of a reader to a book depends largely on the keenness of the reader's imagination; the reaction to a film depends on the vividness of presentation.

Hence many things which might be described or suggested in a book could not possibly be presented in a film.

E. This is also true when comparing the film with the newspaper.

a. Newspapers present by description, films by actual presentation.

b. Newspapers are after the fact and present things as having taken place; the film gives the events in the process of enactment and with apparent reality of life.

F. Everything possible in a play is not possible in a film:

a. Because of the larger audience of the film, and its consequential mixed character. Psychologically, the larger the audience, the lower the moral mass resistance to suggestion.

b. Because through light, enlargement of character, presentation, scenic emphasis, etc., the screen story is brought closer to the audience than the play.

c. The enthusiasm for and interest in the film actors and actresses, developed beyond anything of the sort in history, makes the audience largely sympathetic toward the characters they portray and the stories in which they figure. Hence the audience is more ready to confuse actor and actress and the characters they portray, and it is most receptive of the emotions and ideals presented by the favorite stars.

G. Small communities, remote from sophistication and from the hardening process which often takes place in the ethical and moral standards of larger cities, are easily and readily reached by any sort of film.

H. The grandeur of mass settings, large action, spectacular features, etc., affects and arouses more intensely the emotional side of the audience. In general, the mobility, popularity, accessibility, emotional appeal, vividness, straightforward presentation of fact in the film make for more intimate contact with a larger audience and for greater emotional appeal.

Hence the larger moral responsibilities of the motion pictures.

Reasons Underlying the General Principles

I. No picture shall be produced which will lower the moral standards of those who see it. Hence the sympathy of the audience should never be thrown to the side of crime, wrong-doing, evil or sin. This is done:

1. When evil is made to appear attractive and alluring, and good is made to appear unattractive.

2. When the sympathy of the audience is thrown on the side of crime, wrongdoing, evil, sin. The same is true of a film that would throw sympathy against goodness, honor, innocence, purity or honesty.

Note: Sympathy with a person who sins is not the same as sympathy with the sin or crime of which he is guilty. We may feel sorry for the plight of the murderer or even understand the circumstances which led him to his crime: we may not feel sympathy with the wrong which he has done. The presentation of evil is often essential for art or fiction or drama. This in itself is not wrong provided:

a. That evil is not presented alluringly. Even if later in the film the evil is condemned or punished, it must not be allowed to appear so attractive that the audience's emotions are drawn to desire or approve so strongly that later the condemnation is forgotten and only the apparent joy of sin is remembered.

b. That throughout, the audience feels sure that evil is wrong and good is right.

II. Correct standards of life shall, as far as possible, be presented. A wide knowledge of life and of living is made possible through the film. When right standards are consistently presented, the motion picture exercises the most powerful influences. It builds character, develops right ideals, inculcates correct principles, and all this in attractive story form. If motion pictures consistently hold up for admiration high types of characters and present stories that will affect lives for the better, they can become the most powerful force for the improvement of mankind.

III. Law, natural or human, shall not be ridiculed, nor shall sympathy be created for its violation. By natural law is understood the law which is written in the hearts of all mankind, the greater underlying principles of right and justice dictated by conscience. By human law is understood the law written by civilized nations.

1. The presentation of crimes against the law is often necessary for the carrying out of the plot. But the presentation must not throw

sympathy with the crime as against the law nor with the criminal as against those who punish him.

2. The courts of the land should not be presented as unjust. This does not mean that a single court may not be presented as unjust, much less that a single court official must not be presented this way. But the court system of the country must not suffer as a result of this presentation.

Reasons Underlying the Particular Applications

I. Sin and evil enter into the story of human beings and hence in themselves are valid dramatic material.

II. In the use of this material, it must be distinguished between sin which repels by its very nature, and sins which often attract.

a. In the first class come murder, most theft, many legal crimes, lying, hypocrisy, cruelty, etc.
b. In the second class come sex sins, sins and crimes of apparent heroism, such as banditry, daring thefts, leadership in evil, organized crime, revenge, etc. The first class needs less care in treatment, as sins and crimes of this class are naturally unattractive. The audience instinctively condemns all such and is repelled.

Hence the important objective must be to avoid the hardening of the audience, especially of those who are young and impressionable, to the thought and fact of crime. People can become accustomed even to murder, cruelty, brutality, and repellent crimes, if these are too frequently repeated.

The second class needs great care in handling, as the response of human nature to their appeal is obvious. This is treated more fully below.

III. A careful distinction can be made between films intended for general distribution, and films intended for use in theatres restricted to a limited audience. Themes and plots quite appropriate for the latter would be altogether out of place and dangerous in the former.

Note: The practice of using a general theatre and limiting its patronage to "Adults Only" is not completely satisfactory and is only partially effective.

However, maturer minds may easily understand and accept without harm subject matter in plots which do younger people positive harm.

Hence: If there should be created a special type of theatre, catering exclusively to an adult audience, for plays of this character (plays with problem themes, difficult discussions and maturer treatment) it would seem to afford an outlet, which does not now exist, for pictures unsuitable for general distribution but permissible for exhibitions to a restricted audience.

I. Crimes Against the Law. The treatment of crimes against the law must not:

1. Teach methods of crime.
2. Inspire potential criminals with a desire for imitation.
3. Make criminals seem heroic and justified.

Revenge in modern times shall not be justified. In lands and ages of less developed civilization and moral principles, revenge may sometimes be presented. This would be the case especially in places where no law exists to cover the crime because of which revenge is committed.

Because of its evil consequences, the drug traffic should not be presented in any form. The existence of the trade should not be brought to the attention of audiences.

The use of liquor should never be excessively presented. In scenes from American life, the necessities of plot and proper characterization alone justify its use. And in this case, it should be shown with moderation.

II. Sex: Out of a regard for the sanctity of marriage and the home, the triangle, that is, the love of a third party for one already married, needs careful handling. The treatment should not throw sympathy against marriage as an institution. Scenes of passion must be treated with an honest acknowledgement of human nature and its normal reactions. Many scenes cannot be presented without arousing dangerous emotions on the part of the immature, the young or the criminal classes. Even within the limits of pure love, certain facts have been universally regarded by lawmakers as outside the limits of safe presentation.

In the case of impure love, the love which society has always regarded as wrong and which has been banned by divine law, the following are important:

1. Impure love must not be presented as attractive and beautiful.
2. It must not be the subject of comedy or farce, or treated as material for laughter.
3. It must not be presented in such a way to arouse passion or morbid curiosity on the part of the audience.

4. It must not be made to seem right and permissible.

5. It general, it must not be detailed in method and manner.

III. Vulgarity; IV. Obscenity; V. Profanity; hardly need further explanation than is contained in the Code. VI. Costume

General Principles:

1. The effect of nudity or semi-nudity upon the normal man or woman, and much more upon the young and upon immature persons, has been honestly recognized by all lawmakers and moralists.

2. Hence the fact that the nude or semi-nude body may be beautiful does not make its use in the films moral. For, in addition to its beauty, the effect of the nude or semi-nude body on the normal individual must be taken into consideration.

3. Nudity or semi-nudity used simply to put a "punch" into a picture comes under the head of immoral actions. It is immoral in its effect on the average audience.

4. Nudity can never be permitted as being necessary for the plot. Semi-nudity must not result in undue or indecent exposures.

5. Transparent or translucent materials and silhouette are frequently more suggestive than actual exposure.

VII. Dances
Dancing in general is recognized as an art and as a beautiful form of expressing human emotions.

But dances which suggest or represent sexual actions, whether performed solo or with two or more; dances intended to excite the emotional reaction of an audience; dances with movement of the breasts, excessive body movements while the feet are stationary, violate decency and are wrong.

VIII. Religion

The reason why ministers of religion may not be comic characters or villains is simply because the attitude taken toward them may easily become the attitude taken toward religion in general. Religion is lowered in the minds of the audience because of the lowering of the audience's respect for a minister.

IX. Locations

Certain places are so closely and thoroughly associated with sexual life or with sexual sin that their use must be carefully limited.

X. National Feelings

The just rights, history, and feelings of any nation are entitled to most careful consideration and respectful treatment.

XI. Titles

As the title of a picture is the brand on that particular type of goods, it must conform to the ethical practices of all such honest business.

XII. Repellent Subjects

Such subjects are occasionally necessary for the plot. Their treatment must never offend good taste nor injure the sensibilities of an audience.

APPENDIX B

Advertising Code

These additions and modifications are attributed to the ascension of Joseph I. Breen to head the Production Code in 1934:

1. We subscribe to the Code of Business Ethics of the International Advertising Association, based on "truth, honesty, and integrity."
2. Good taste shall be the guiding rule.
3. Illustration and text in advertising shall faithfully represent the pictures themselves.
4. No false or misleading statement shall be used directly or implied.
5. No text or illustration shall ridicule or tend to ridicule any religion or religious faith.
6. The history, institution and nationalities of all countries shall be represented with all fairness.
7. Profanity and vulgarity shall be avoided.
8. Pictorial and copy treatment of officers of the law shall not be of such a nature as to undermine authority.
9. Specific details of crime, inciting imitation, shall not be used.
10. Motion picture advertisers shall bear in mind the provision of the Production Code that use of liquor in American life be restricted to the necessities of characterization and plot.
11. Nudity with meretricious purpose, and salacious postures, shall not be used.

Modifications and Expansions of the Production Code of Ethics:

I-3. The illegal drug traffic must not be portrayed in such a way as to stimulate curiosity concerning the use of, or traffic in, such drugs; nor shall scenes be approved which show the use of, or the effects of illegal drugs in detail.

V. No approval by the Production Code Administration shall be given to the use of words and phrases in motion pictures including, but not limited to, the following:

Alley-cat (applied to a woman)
Bat (applied to a woman)
Broad (applied to a woman)
"Bronx Cheer" (the sound)
Chippie
Cocotte
Cripes
Fanny
Fairy (in a vulgar sense)
Fire—cries of
Gawd
God, Lord, Jesus, Christ (unless used reverently)
Goose (in a vulgar sense)
"Hold your Hat" (or "hats")
Hot (applied to a woman)
"in your hat"

APPENDIX B

Louse

Lousy

Madam (relating to prostitution)

Nance

Nerts/Nertz

Nuts (except when meaning crazy)

Pansy

Razzberry (the sound)

Slut (applied to a woman)

S.O.B.

Son-of-a

Tart

Toilet gags

Tom-cat (applied to a man)

Traveling salesman and Farmer's daughter jokes

Whore

Damn, Hell (excepting where the use of said last two words shall
be essential and required for portrayal, in proper historical context,
of any scene or dialogue based upon historical fact or folklore, or
for the presentation in proper literary context of a Biblical, or other
religious, quotation, or a quotation from a literary work, provided
that no such use be permitted which is intrinsically objectionable or
offense good taste).

In the administration of Section V of the Production Code, the Production Code Administration may take cognizance of the fact that the

following words and phrases are obviously offensive to the patrons of motion pictures, in the United States, and more particularly to patrons of motion pictures in foreign countries: Chink, Dago, Frog, Greaser, Hunkie, Kike, Nigger, Spic, Wop, Yid.

Code Blue!

A Comedy in Two Acts

Arnie Reisman & Nat Segaloff

Code Blue!

A Comedy in Two Acts

by Arnie Reisman & Nat Segaloff

The Settings:

Preminger-Herbert Productions Offices
Chasen's Restaurant
Production Code Administration Offices
Darryl F. Zanuck's dining room at Twentieth Century-Fox studios
Hedda Hopper's Alcove Office
Legion of Decency Office
Martin J. Quigley's Office
Monsignor Patrick J. Masterson's Office
Coffee shop

The Characters:

Joseph Breen, age 65, the fulminating head of the Production Code Administration

Otto Preminger, age 48, the Teutonic director

Jack Metzger, age 26, up-and-coming Code assistant

Emily Doakes, age 23, the new kid, secretary

Darryl F. Zanuck, age 51, diminutive but powerful head of Twentieth Century-Fox

Hedda Hopper, age 68, gossip columnist, famous for hats

F. Hugh Herbert, age 56, German-born playwright and wit

Monsignor Patrick J. Masterson, SJ, age 43, the cleric behind the Legion of Decency

Martin J. Quigley, age 63, trade paper publisher and secret author of the Code

The action takes place in Hollywood, California, in 1953–1954 before, during, and after the production of *The Moon Is Blue*.

Note: Please keep in mind that *Code Blue!* contains exposition for the audience of the play that readers of *Breaking the Code* will not need.

ACT ONE

ACT 1, SCENE 1—PREMINGER-HERBERT PRODUCTIONS OFFICE

In the process of being closed. A one sheet for the stage production of *The Moon Is Blue* hangs off-center. Papers are boxed for storage.

F. HUGH HERBERT is cleaning out the desk, jogging papers, etc. Something catches his eye. He looks around to make sure he's not being spied upon.

HERBERT: "Virgin." There, I said it. "Virgin." (*pause*) "Seduce." (*pause*) "Pregnant." (*He checks for any reaction. None.*) I didn't think so. Unless I missed it, those three little words didn't just bring down civilization. But they very nearly brought down Hollywood. That was in 1953 when our little immorality tale is set—though it really began in 1927 when the studios created the "Production Code" to fight a growing public reaction to screen smut. In other words, instead of risking Congress censoring movies, the movies censored themselves. The Production Code was run by a former U.S. Postmaster General named Will Hays, who looked like an ear of corn. The Hays Office, as it was called, censored not only movies but short subjects, cartoons, previews, and advertising. For seven years the studios patted them on the head and ignored them. Until 1934 when Hays hired Joseph Breen to enforce the Production Code. Breen took to it like a preacher to sin, and for twenty years nobody challenged his decisions on what you could—but usually couldn't—put on the screen. Then came Otto Preminger, and that's where I come in. The characters you're about to meet are real, and so is the story. Well, I may've changed a couple of things here and there; I'm the writer. And sometimes the referee.

SOUND: A fight BELL, then ARENA AMBIENCE.

A microphone descends and HERBERT talks into it.

HERBERT: Laaaadies and Gentlemen! In this corner, standing five foot ten, weighing in at two hundred fighting Irish pounds, the head of the Hollywood Production Code Administration and the man who has his finger firmly up the pulse of the public: Joseph Ignatius Breen!

JOSEPH I. BREEN is a burly Irishman with sparkling eyes and a quick mind. Don't let his boxer's stance fool you; he's bright as well as belligerent.

BREEN: (*posturing*) The vulgar, the cheap, and the tawdry is OUT! There is no place on the screen for pictures which offend against common decency, and these the motion picture industry will not allow!

HERBERT: In this corner, standing six foot one, with the weight of the world on his shoulders, whose hits include *Laura* and *Forever Amber* and who will soon be acting in Billy Wilder's *Stalag 17*, the director you love to hate and the producer you hate to love: Otto Preminger!

OTTO PREMINGER is tall and well-groomed and has a shaved head. He is Viennese and charming but also mercurial.

PREMINGER: I am not a crusader, but it gives me great pleasure to fight for my rights. If you don't fight, you lose them. Because if the right to free expression deteriorates, that is the first step to dictatorship, to totalitarian government, to an America I did not come running to with my arms wide open.

HERBERT: And lurking behind the scenes—invisible to the naked eye but not to the naked body—weighing in at a circulation of twenty thousand including all the studio heads, politicians, and church

Credit: Collection Christophel/Alamy Stock Photo

David Niven, Maggie McNamara, and William Holden in *The Moon Is Blue*, 1953. *Credit*: United Artists/Photofest © United Artists

David Niven, star of *The Moon Is Blue*. *Credit*: By Allan Warren— Own work allanwarren.com, CC BY-SA 3.0/Wikimedia Commons

William Holden, star of *The Moon Is Blue. Credit*: Photofest

Maggie McNamara and William Holden in *The Moon Is Blue. Credit*: United Artists/ Photofest © United Artists

Credit: Photofest

Frank Sinatra and Kim Novak in *The Man with the Golden Arm*. *Credit*: United Artists/ Photofest © United Artists

Frank Sinatra in *The Man with the Golden Arm*. *Credit*: United Artists/ Photofest © United Artists

Title design by Saul Bass. Preminger used Bass for the rest of his films, including some that died in pre-production. *Credit*: By Saul Bass/ Wikimedia Commons

Anatomy of a Murder (1959), directed by Otto Preminger. L–R: James Stewart (as Paul Biegler), Joseph N. Welch (as Judge Weaver), Lee Remick (as Laura Manion), George C. Scott (as Asst. State Atty. Gen. Claude Dancer). *Credit*: Columbia Pictures/Photofest © Columbia Pictures

Credit: Columbia Pictures/Photofest © Columbia Pictures

Will Geer (left) and Charles Laughton (center) in *Advise & Consent*. It would be Laughton's last film and Geer's first after having been blacklisted. *Credit*: By Columbia Pictures/Wikimedia Commons

(L–R) Charles Laughton, George Grizzard, Edward Andrews, Walter Pidgeon, and production assistant David DeSilva in *Advise & Consent*. *Credit*: By It&#039, CC By-SA 4.0 / Wikimedia Commons

Will H. Hays, formal, president of Motion Picture Producers and Distributors of America (MPPDA). *Credit*: By Harris & Ewing, photographer—Library of Congress Catalog (PD)

(L–R) Will Hays, Darryl Zanuck, Joseph Schenck, and Adolph Zukor at a dinner honoring Zukor's twenty-fifth anniversary as a movie producer, 1937. *Credit*: Photofest

Joseph I. Breen, head of the Production Code Administration (late 1930s). *Credit*: Photofest

Martin J. Quigley (left), publisher of the *Motion Picture Herald* and secret force behind both the Production Code and the Legion of Decency (Martin Quigley, Carter DeHaven, December 1920). *Credit*: Historic Collection/Alamy Stock Photo

Jack Valenti, president of the MPAA and creator of the present movie rating system. *Credit*: By John Matthew Smith, CC By-SA 2.0 / Wikimedia Commons

Henry Kissinger and Jack Valenti at the Academy Awards, circa 1980. *Credit*: Photofest

Otto Preminger. *Credit*: By Allan Warren—Own work, CC BY-SA 3.0/Wikimedia Commons

Arthur Krim, president of United Artists *Credit*: United Artists/ Photofest © United Artists

Screen credit for the first film given a Production Code Seal, *The World Moves On*, 1934. *Credit*: Author's collection

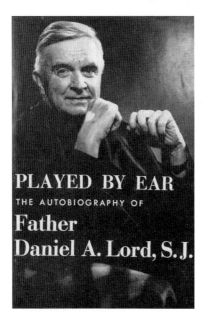

Father Daniel A. Lord, S.J., who cowrote the Production Code, on the cover of one of his many books. *Credit*: Author's collection

Fatima, the hoochie-koochie dancer from the 1896 Chicago Exposition: original and censored versions. *Credit*: Author's collection

groups—publisher of the *Motion Picture Herald*, Martin J. Quigley!

MARTIN J. QUIGLEY is a worm but still smooth enough to appear cordial. He actually wears a villain's thin moustache.

QUIGLEY: This isn't just about dirty words, it's about dirty thoughts. As a publisher and a Catholic I've fought a long, hard, and stiff battle against the insertion of smut. I see a Legion of Decency spreading wide the studio doors. And thrusting deep into Hollywood's dark passages. Cleaning up the movies will be the—the—the climax!—of my—mission.

SOUND: Bell rings again. Crowds cheer, then fade.

HERBERT: And it all started one year ago in this very office.

BREEN and QUIGLEY exit. OTTO removes his jacket and joins HER-BERT, who is now tacking up the poster.

ACT 1, SCENE 2—THE SAME—A YEAR EARLIER

OTTO: We have good news! Everything is arranged!

HERBERT: Bravo, Otto, that is wonderful! Good work!

OTTO: Krim says he is completely behind us. All we need do is assemble the right cast.

HERBERT: What's a Krim?

OTTO: Arthur Krim, head of United Artists. Is there another kind?

HERBERT: United Artists makes movies.

OTTO: They do, indeed.

HERBERT: Since when are we making a movie?

OTTO: What else do I do with a Broadway hit that I directed?

HERBERT: Stage another one.

OTTO: Not when the first one can bring us back to Hollywood.

HERBERT: Go back? I've only just unpacked here.

OTTO: Good. That will save time.

HERBERT: Hold on, Otto. You said we'd do *The Moon Is Blue* and then my next one.

OTTO: All in good time, Hugh. Why do you think I went to such effort to stage *The Moon Is Blue* in the first place?

HERBERT: You said you liked my script.

OTTO: Yes, but I also knew that if we made a success here in New York, we could go back to California and name our own terms.

HERBERT: What about *Kiss and Tell*? I thought that was our next—

OTTO: Theatre is where you go between pictures. *The Moon Is Blue* has given us power in Hollywood. We must use it.

HERBERT: Two hits in a row would be better than one hit in a row, especially if I've written them both.

OTTO: Where is your self-confidence? You are Frederick Hugh Herbert the playwright! *The Moon Is Blue* ran for over two years to sold-out houses! Why do you want to risk it with something called *Kiss and Tell*?

HERBERT: Why don't I stay in New York and write for the theatre during the day. At night I can write for television.

OTTO: Television? If you want to be a whore, go to Eighth Avenue.

HERBERT: Broadway's fine for me. On Broadway the playwright is king. In Hollywood, writers are just what Jack Warner calls us: schmucks with Underwoods.

OTTO: Even with a hit play, in New York the best you can be is a junior schmuck. Success travels west like the sun, and so must we.

HERBERT: And just how were you planning to get *The Moon Is Blue* past the Production Code? That's why we did it on stage in the first place.

OTTO: Joe Breen respects my integrity.

HERBERT: It will take more than integrity to get *The Moon Is Blue* past the Breen Office.

OTTO: Alas, I know. What good is having enormous integrity without the talent to match?

HERBERT: Oh, stop being Otto Preminger. My agent sent the script around the studios a year ago and everybody passed.

OTTO: A year ago? Why was I not told?

HERBERT: You weren't directing it. Anyway, I'm telling you now. He slipped it on the q.t. to Warners and Paramount, and Warners and Paramount slipped it on the q'er t to the Breen Office. And Joe Breen himself shot it down with both barrels. He said that under no circumstances will *The Moon Is Blue* get a Production Code Seal of Approval. And you know what a Code Seal means.

OTTO: The public's guarantee of the finest in screen banality.

HERBERT: Grandstand as much as you want, Otto, but you know without a Seal a movie can't be released, and our *Moon* sets slowly in the East River. That's why I'm staying in New York.

OTTO: The visionary has always faced opposition from ignorance! America is growing up. Hollywood is changing. Independence, Hugh, independence!

HERBERT: Bankruptcy, Otto, bankruptcy! What are you, the John Adams of Hollywood?

OTTO: If the studios won't make our film, we shall make it ourselves. We have no overhead—

HERBERT: — we have no assets—

OTTO: — we have no expenses—

HERBERT: — we have no collateral—

OTTO: — we have no debts—

HERBERT: — we have no income, we have no security, we have no—

OTTO: (sharply)—guts! Look at the studios. They are under Supreme Court orders to sell off their theatre chains and compete like everybody else. You and I can be the "everybody else"! This is the age of independent companies like United Artists! We can use the play's future royalties as collateral, defer our salaries, have the actors also defer, and hire the crew for scale.

HERBERT: And my uncle has a barn where we can put on a show.

OTTO: We can even shoot a German version at the same time and presell the foreign market to get some of our money back early.

HERBERT is momentarily beaten.

HERBERT: You've been planning this all along?

OTTO: It's thinking ahead. The future is ours, Hugh, but we have to fight for it. No one believes in censorship. It may be au courant in Hollywood, but it's un-American everywhere else. The press will be on our side. We must give them someone to cheer for.

HERBERT: And that would be us?

OTTO: Who better?

HERBERT: The Breen Office has already said *The Moon Is Blue* will never get a Code Seal. What chance would Herbert-Preminger Productions have?

OTTO: You let Preminger-Herbert Productions worry about that.

HERBERT: Yes, but I'll be one half of Herbert-Preminger Productions.

OTTO: And I am the other half. One of the advantages of being Otto Preminger is that I am Otto Preminger.

OTTO preens, and HERBERT regards him.

OTTO (cont'd): We will be Preminger-Herbert Productions. Besides, I have more letters in my name than you do.

HERBERT: Ever hear of Rodgers and Hammerstein?

OTTO: What about Currier and Ives?

HERBERT: Marx and Engels!

OTTO: Leopold and Loeb!

HERBERT: Sears and Roebuck!

OTTO: Abercrombie & Fitch!

HERBERT: Who's on first? (suddenly it hits him) Achtung! You don't just want to film *The Moon Is Blue*. You want to take on Joe Breen. You want to challenge the whole Production Code—with my play! My little baby! It never hurt anyone!

OTTO: Don't you see? *The Moon Is Blue* is the perfect weapon. Two years on Broadway—three road companies—and not one censorship protest anywhere. Billy Graham couldn't do better!

HERBERT: Well, I don't know—

OTTO: If it were pornography we would have no case. But you have written a moral tale where the only filth is in the mind of the viewer. We will defeat the Production Code with Joe Breen's own self-righteousness! We will free motion pictures from the yoke of censorship!

HERBERT: We will lose our shirts and become pariahs. My name will be mud! Do you hear? MUD.

OTTO: "Mud" is still shorter than "Preminger."

HERBERT has to concede, but not without one last caution.

HERBERT: If Breen wins, the Production Code will be stronger than
ever.

OTTO: You worry too much, Hugh. After all, it's only a movie.

OTTO crosses to his next position as HERBERT talks to the audience.

HERBERT: Next stop: California—as Otto proceeded to charm
the least charming person in Hollywood. The place: Chasen's
Restaurant. The person? Medusa, better known as Hedda Hopper,
the nationally syndicated gossip columnist and Wicked Witch of
the West Coast.

HERBERT exits.

ACT 1, SCENE 3—CHASEN'S

OTTO and HEDDA HOPPER—compact and feline—inhabit a banquette. Every time we see HEDDA she will be wearing a different outrageous hat. For now she is taking notes as OTTO speaks.

HEDDA: What I don't understand, Otto, is how you could've refused to renew your studio contract from Darryl F. Zanuck, go to New York, and take a pay cut.

OTTO (*grandly*): I wanted to return to my roots in the live theatre. And what better way to do so than with a comedy of manners about American attitudes toward seduction?

HEDDA laughs.

OTTO (cont'd): I am being serious, Hedda!

HEDDA: Oh, come on, Otto. What's German for *stier sheitzen*?

OTTO: All right, I give up. There is no fooling Hedda Hopper.

HEDDA: And there's no ignoring Otto Preminger. So let's bury the Wiener schnitzel and tell me why you've come all the way to Hollywood just to buy me lunch.

OTTO: I am going to make a film of *The Moon Is Blue*.

HEDDA: Joe Breen will never give you a Production Code seal.

OTTO: Well, in that case, I will not make the film. Thanks, Hedda. (*to WAITER*) Check please!

HEDDA: Oh, now, now, come on, sweetie! There's more to it than that. We're still on my first drink.

OTTO snaps his fingers and motions o.s. for another round.

OTTO: It is a matter of free speech, Hedda, dear. This is bigger than Breen. We are talking about the First Amendment, which must be defended and protected. I am not trying to be the white knight, but I'm not going to open the door for another little Hitler to take over . . . or Stalin. Movie audiences deserve better.

HEDDA: I'm not a jury, Otto. I know you used to be a lawyer in Germany.

OTTO (*quickly*): — Austria—

HEDDA: — before the Anschluss. This is a matter of decency. We all believe in free speech, but sometimes it goes too far.

OTTO: How would you like it if someone told you what to print?

HEDDA: They wouldn't dare! But I never print anything lewd or vulgar. The First Amendment wasn't made to protect filth.

OTTO: There is nothing lewd or vulgar in *The Moon Is Blue.* It's a simple boy-meets-girl story. He wants to seduce her, she says no. All that happens is that nothing happens.

HEDDA: I wouldn't pay to see that, and I get in for free.

OTTO: Ah, but it is all in how the "nothing" happens that something happens.

HEDDA: You say it isn't dirty?

OTTO: Schmutz is in the eye of the beholder, and one man's schmutz is another man's theatre.

HEDDA: I'll be the judge!

OTTO: Don't let Joe Breen hear that! He wants to be the judge, jury, and the artistic executioner.

HEDDA: Oh stop it, Otto. The industry needs Joe Breen. You can't put just anything up on the screen. That's what brought on the call for the Code in the first place.

OTTO: That was thirty years ago! The country's grown up. World War Two! Korea! Movies are shown in a building, and any usher can tell you nobody gets in a theatre by accident.

HEDDA: The Breen Office protects family values. Are you against family values?

OTTO (*pontificating*): Since when is censorship a family value? It's un-American!

HEDDA: What's your angle, Otto?

OTTO (*holier-than-thou*): Angle?

HEDDA: What's your scheme? I want to hear alllll about it. I've got my pencil and pad sharpened, and as soon as we get the waiter's attention—

OTTO (*barking*): ACHTUNG!

Hedda jumps.

HEDDA: Please! The man may still have family in the old country!

Otto calls o.s. to the Waiter.

OTTO: Bring Miss Hopper's highball! *Mach schnell.* (*sweetly*) If you please. (*charming to Hedda, if not lubricious*) And now, dear Hedda, here is the story. Or the "scoop" as you professional journalists call it. About how a bright young man from AUSTRIA came to Hollywood, made a great success, and now finds himself a poor, innocent David going up against the Goliath of the Production

Code. His slingshot is *The Moon Is Blue*—a comedy that's as clean and sweet as the Los Angeles air.

Lights dim and then fade up on:

ACT 1, SCENE 4—PRODUCTION CODE ADMINISTRATION OFFICES

EMILY DOAKES sits at a desk while JACK METZGER paces beside her, dictating as she takes the shorthand.

JACK: Bitch.

EMILY: Yeah.

JACK: Slut.

EMILY: Yeah.

JACK: Tart.

EMILY: With an "E"?

JACK: No, just "tart."

EMILY: As in sour?

JACK: As in alley cat, farmer's daughter, whore—

EMILY: Slow down! Slow down!

JACK: Cocotte. (*note: pronounced ko-KOTT*)

EMILY: What?

JACK: Cocotte.

EMILY: What's a cocotte?

JACK: A prostitute. Nobody uses it; I had to look it up.

EMILY: If nobody uses it, why do we censor it?

JACK: In case they ever do.

EMILY: You're nuts.

JACK: You can't say that either.

EMILY: What's wrong with nuts?

JACK: Not if they're a man's. Only if it means crazy.

EMILY: It's all crazy, if you ask me.

JACK: Once again, Miss Doakes, the Production Code has a list of words you cannot say on the screen. If you're going to work here, you have to learn them.

EMILY: All on my first day?

JACK: Keep writing.

EMILY: My pen gets stuck on the dirty ones.

JACK: "Bat," applied to a woman. "Broad," applied to a woman. "Chippie" applied to a woman. "Hot" applied to a woman—

EMILY: Doesn't anything around here ever apply to a man?

JACK: "Fairy," "nance," "pansy" and "homo." They all come under sex perversion.

EMILY: Did somebody actually sit down and make up this list or just scrape it off a bathroom wall?

JACK: No bathrooms! That is, no toilets.

EMILY: Then where do people go?

JACK: Television. Keep writing.

EMILY: That's lousy.

JACK: Can't say that either: "louse," "lousy," or "nertz."

EMILY: What's "Nertz"?

JACK: Nobody knows, but you can't say it.

EMILY: Like cocotte?

JACK: Now you're catching on.

EMILY: I had an aunt once.

JACK: Is there more to this story?

EMILY: She talked dirty.

JACK: Somebody shoulda spanked her—

EMILY: — Fanny. Her name was Fanny.

This gets JACK's attention.

EMILY (cont'd): Her name was Fanny and she talked because the men she worked with in the factory gave her more respect.

JACK: I wouldn't've.

EMILY: You didn't know my Fanny.

JACK: Shall we continue? "Damn" and "Hell" may never be used except where they are essential for portraying historical fact or folklore.

EMILY: "Damn the torpedoes!"

JACK: "Hell hath no fury like a woman scorned."

EMILY: The quick brown fox jumped over the lazy dog.

JACK: The Production Code also realizes that the following words or phrases offend certain ethnic groups: Chink, Dago, Frog, Greaser, Hunkie, Kike, Nigger, Spic, Wop, Yid.

EMILY: Has it ever occurred to anyone that the Production Code itself is offensive?

JACK: Are you getting it all down?

EMILY: Yeah, but it's hard to swallow. You mean none of those words can be used in movies?

JACK: Not since 1934. It's the job of this office to keep motion pictures clean. Any film that gets our Seal of Approval is safe for the whole family. Like milk or Wheaties. Without a Code Seal no theatre will show it and no newspaper will advertise it.

EMILY: I can see this is going to be a challenging job, Mr. Metzger.

JACK: We're not film critics here, Miss Doakes. The Production Code Administration keeps the screen wholesome. If you only knew the stuff we had to cut out of movies that are now considered classics!

EMILY: Like what?

JACK: Like in *Casablanca*. Claude Rains originally told Humphrey Bogart, "You enjoy war, I enjoy women." We made them change it to "You like war, I like women."

EMILY: There's a difference between enjoying something and liking it?

JACK: In the original script it's pretty clear that Rains makes women sleep with him to get their exit visas. We were shocked, shocked! to hear that adultery was going on!

EMILY: So the difference between liking and enjoying is . . . ?

JACK: If you enjoy something, it implies sex.

EMILY: I enjoy ice cream.

JACK: In *Bride of Frankenstein* they referred to making a mate for the monster. A "mate" for the monster! We had them change it to "companion." "Mate" means sex. A companion is just—just—

EMILY: "Liking" monsters.

JACK: In *Going My Way*—

EMILY: Oh, really! Priests?

JACK: Father FitzGibbon says, "I will not permit Three Blind Mice to come between me and my God."

EMILY: He was enjoying mice?

JACK: It was objectionable.

EMILY: Were the mice consenting?

JACK: We never make fun of clergy. Can you imagine a priest doing anything wrong?

EMILY: Gee, Mr. Metzger, the Production Code sounds pretty complicated. You don't need a secretary, you need the FBI.

JACK: We don't catch it all, though. In *A Night at the Opera* when Groucho Marx and Margaret Dumont board the ocean liner, she says, "Are you sure you have everything, Otis?" Groucho says, "I haven't had any complaints yet." We missed that one. But the New York state censors didn't.

EMILY: I had no idea filmmakers were so sneaky!

JACK: That's why all of us have to memorize this list of "Don'ts and Be Carefuls." It's our job to see that nothing gets on the screen that offends anyone.

EMILY: What about people who are offended by stupidity?

Joseph I. Breen enters the room—rather, explodes into it—his engine already running. He answers Emily.

BREEN: They don't go to movies, little lady. They read books and listen to radio shows that don't have sponsors. What's progressive in live theatre is indecent on the screen. Jack, who is this charming young thing who asks too many questions?

JACK: This is Emily Doakes. I've pretty much decided she's our new secretary. Miss Doakes, this is Joseph I. Breen, President of the Production Code Administration of the Motion Picture Association of America.

BREEN: How do you do, my dear?

EMILY: Fine, thank you, Mr. Breen. Mr. Metzger was just dictating the list of "Don'ts and Be Carefuls." It's a lot to remember.

BREEN: And it's growing all the time. You wouldn't believe how much slang finds its way into pictures these days. Disgraceful!

EMILY: Where does it all come from?

BREEN: Oh, the usual places. Detective stories. Pool halls. Jazz clubs. You know where to find the most filth? Comic books. Beatniks and comic books. (*prompting*) Did you tell her our in-house motto, Jack?

JACK (*reciting*): "A censor has to have the dirtiest mind—and the cleanest mouth—in the room."

EMILY: I understood that one of the job requirements was that I don't embarrass easily.

BREEN: You don't?

EMILY: I had four brothers.

BREEN: None of us around here has the luxury of blushing, Miss Doakes. Good taste isn't pretty. When it comes to freedom of speech versus freedom of the box office, Hollywood knows what sells tickets. Then we take it out.

EMILY: Does that mean I have the job?

BREEN: If Jack says so.

JACK: I do.

BREEN: And you want it?

EMILY: I do.

BREEN: Then I now pronounce you censor and secretary. Any messages?

JACK shuffles through some pink message slips.

JACK: Jack Warner's angry at us for toning down the drag number in *Calamity Jane*. He agreed to the cuts, but he stuck in a lesbian song.

EMILY: Excuse me: a lesbian song in a Doris Day musical?

JACK: It goes, "Once I had a secret love . . ."

EMILY: I'm beginning to appreciate the value of a dirty mind.

JACK: And a sharp eye. It was Mr. Breen who discovered that Carmen Miranda wasn't wearing underwear in *The Gang's All Here*.

EMILY: He can look behind the screen?

JACK: You know, where she wears the pineapple on her head and sings "The Girl with the Tutti-Fruiti Hat"? She does a kick-turn, her dress goes up, and—and—and —

EMILY: And what?

BREEN: And they grow an awful lot of coffee in Brazil.

JACK: The toughest job we've had lately is censoring *From Here to Eternity*.

EMILY: The bestseller that takes place during Pearl Harbor? I read it. It's pure sex.

BREEN: Impure sex, but go ahead.

JACK: Five drafts later, when Deborah Kerr tells Burt Lancaster on the beach, "I never knew it could be like this," she'd didn't know what "it" was.

BREEN sorts through a stack of scripts on a desk.

BREEN: The price of purity is eternal vigilance.

JACK: *Seven Brides for Seven Brothers*. Rewrite. Seven boys and seven girls get snowed in together for the winter. We told 'em to remove all the hanky-panky.

BREEN: They cut the hanky but added more panky.

EMILY: Is that *The Country Girl* by Clifford Odets? I saw the play. It was so wonderful: an alcoholic actor trying to make a comeback. It was another *Lost Weekend*.

BREEN: Which coulda been better without all the drinking.

JACK: Drinking is a variable. We permitted it in *A Star Is Born*, because Norman Maine commits suicide at the end.

EMILY: Suicide is a mortal sin!

BREEN: Very good. But the way he does it, it's not suicide-suicide, it's a sacrifice-suicide so his wife can be free. It's moral suicide.

EMILY: I'm getting confused.

BREEN: It'll make sense after a while. See, we don't really censor. We just force filmmakers to be creative instead of procreative. (*remembers something*) Look at the time! I have to be at Fox in fifteen minutes. I'll be having lunch with Darryl F. Zanuck, Miss Doakes. The private phone number's in the file, but under no circumstances are you to use it—unless, of course, it's the end of the world.

EMILY: Yes, sir.

BREEN: Hold the fort, Jack. I'll be back in a couple hours.

BREEN leaves.

JACK: Okay we have a couple hours.

EMILY: For what?

JACK: Well, first I can show you around the office—how we file things.

EMILY: First? As in before second?

JACK: Second would be asking you to lunch.

EMILY: First things first, Mr. Metzger. Isn't that why they're numbered?

JACK: Our procedure here is simple, but the process is not. Does that make any sense?

EMILY: If you have to ask, the answer is no.

JACK: It's essential that we track every script that comes through this office. Writers are sneaky and sometimes change things we've okayed, so we're always making comparisons. When a script arrives it gets logged and covered.

EMILY: Covered?

JACK: Synopsized—so if they change the title we can still recognize the material. Consistency is what makes the Production Code effective. No matter who does the work, all the letters go out over Mr. Breen's signature. We try to be diplomatic but the producer still has to do what we say.

EMILY: Or there's no Code seal and the film can't be released.

JACK: You're catching on.

EMILY: If your word is law, why be nice about it?

JACK: The studios pay our keep.

EMILY: This is too much on an empty stomach. That lunch is a good idea, Mr. Metzger.

JACK: Call me Jack. After all, we're in the sex and violence removal business together, and I'm already calling you Emily.

EMILY: It's proper for a boss to call his secretary by her first name. Did you have another reason?

JACK: No, but what if I did?

EMILY: You'll find it under "Don'ts and Be Carefuls."

JACK: (*laughs amiably*) I have a hunch you're gonna fit right in around here.

Lights dim and then raise on:

ACT 1, SCENE 5—DARRYL F. ZANUCK'S DINING ROOM

DARRYL F. ZANUCK is small but has stature—big cigar, bad teeth, and a Midwest-flat tongue. He and BREEN are at lunch in his office.

ZANUCK: You know me, Joe. I'm not a man given to wild exaggeration. That's for the other studio heads, not DFZ. But I predict that CinemaScope will change the world. When *The Robe* opens later this year it's going to make a fortune.

BREEN: Open any robe on screen and you could make a fortune.

ZANUCK: Cute, Joe, cute. But I mean it. Every picture we make from now on is going to be in CinemaScope.

BREEN: Every picture?

ZANUCK: In the future we don't want stories with depth, we want stories with width.

BREEN: Which brings up your new starlet: Marilyn Monroe. You're really building her up.

ZANUCK: She's already built. Like bricks.

BREEN: In her new film her bricks get wet.

ZANUCK: It's called *Niagara*. Like the falls.

BREEN: Which is what they practically do out of her dress. You know you can't show that, Darryl. All she's wearing underneath is makeup.

ZANUCK: You didn't have any Code problems with Monroe and Jane Russell in *How to Marry a Millionaire*.

BREEN: That's because the camera couldn't get close enough without them poking the lens out. Besides, dramas are more serious than musicals.

ZANUCK: You're being inconsistent.

BREEN: It's perfectly consistent: I know it when I see it.

ZANUCK : Maybe it's time to give the Code another look, Joe. It's been, what, nineteen years since Will Hays hired you to enforce it? How long can Hollywood keep its virginity?

BREEN: As long as there are groups like the Catholic Legion of Decency and publishers like Martin Quigley, that's how long.

ZANUCK: Please, not while I'm eating!

BREEN: Martin's a friend. He helped write the Code and didn't want credit for it. Any time anybody so much as mentions changing the Code, we get it from Quigley and the Church both.

ZANUCK: Back when David Selznick wanted to use "damn" at the end of *Gone with the Wind* you found him a loophole. You said it was, quote, "vulgar but not obscene," and compared Margaret Mitchell's book to the Bible.

BREEN: But we also fined him five thousand dollars and he pretended to be contrite. But that was *Gone with the Wind*, not *Niagara*.

> SOUND: *Zanuck's private phone rings.*

ZANUCK: Are you expecting a call?

BREEN: Certainly not.

> *Zanuck answers the phone.*

ZANUCK: What is it? (*Zanuck goes ashen*) What? Who let her in? Stop her. I don't care, shoot her. No, I guess you can't.

He slams the phone into its cradle.

ZANUCK: Brace yourself. It's Hedda.

Hedda Hopper storms in with another hat.

HEDDA: You thought you could hide from me!

ZANUCK: Always happy to see you, Hedda. Love the hat.

HEDDA: You're just saying that, Darryl, sweetie; give us a big kiss anyway. Mmmmmwah!

They kiss air as Breen watches.

HEDDA (cont'd): That wasn't so bad, was it?

BREEN (*sotto voce*): You kissed the wrong end.

HEDDA: What?

BREEN: Nothing.

ZANUCK: Hedda, you know Joe Breen.

HEDDA: That's why I'm here. I'd kiss you, too, but what would the censors say?

BREEN: I've been kissed, Hedda. I have six kids.

HEDDA: Joe, some new girl in your office wouldn't tell me where to find you. I want her fired.

BREEN: You found me anyway.

HEDDA: I have my sources.

ZANUCK: A little birdie in your hat?

HEDDA: A little spy at your studio. Now, then, Joe: I just had lunch with Otto Preminger.

BREEN: And how is my old friend?

HEDDA: Save the hooey for Lolly Parsons. Preminger says he sent you the screenplay for *The Moon Is Blue* and you rejected it.

BREEN: That's a confidential matter.

HEDDA: As it should be. Tell me anyway.

BREEN: It's our job, Hedda. Producers serve, we return. They thrust, we parry. It's all part of the creative process.

HEDDA (*skeptical*): Mmm-hmm. Well, parry this: Preminger says he doesn't care what the Production Code wants, he's going to shoot *The Moon Is Blue* as is and—let me get the quote right—(*German accent*) "The Standards of the studios are based on the interpretation of an antiquated Code. I shall make the picture without compromise or not at all."

ZANUCK: Yep, that sounds like Otto.

HEDDA: I'm not finished. Quote (*German again*): "If the Code or any other group or individual should try to interfere with our right to offer 'The Moon Is Blue' to the American public, we shall take every possible step provided by law to protect ourselves. Neither I nor writer F. Hugh Herbert wishes to be crusaders or martyrs, but we must defend ourselves when attacked." Vell?

ZANUCK: Vell!

BREEN: Vell, vell!

HEDDA: I'm on deadline.

BREEN (*measured*): All right, Hedda, take this down. Quote: The Code was written by the producers and has been administered and amended by them since 1934. It represents the best interests of the motion picture industry and the American people.

There is a pause you could drive Hedda's ego through.

HEDDA: C'mon, Joe, gimme something that doesn't sound like you're sitting on a table leg.

BREEN: Off the record?

HEDDA: You can trust me.

BREEN: He just loves you for your ink.

HEDDA: Oh, I know that! You think I have "idiot" stenciled on my hat? The play's hot stuff. A Broadway smash.

BREEN: That's the legitimate stage. Movies are illegitimate. People go to movies who've never seen a Broadway show—who've never been to a big city, even. Who've never met a Democrat.

HEDDA: This guy Hugh Herbert. What do we know about him?

BREEN: F. Hugh?

HEDDA: I beg your pardon!

BREEN: His name's Frederick Hugh Herbert. Another German. He goes by his first F. He's written pictures here, and every now and then he writes a play.

HEDDA: Lots of plays become movies. They always get changed.

BREEN: And so will this. It's a long way from script to screen. We base our final decision on the finished film, and Mr. Preminger is a professional and a good American—for a German. He'll do the right thing eventually.

HEDDA: This burns your hide, doesn't it, Joe?

BREEN: Not at all. I have God and the Code behind me. In that order.

HEDDA: I hear Preminger's a Hollywood liberal.

BREEN: Is he a Commie?

HEDDA: Worse: he an artiste. But that's just gossip, and gossip's for shopgirls and stockbrokers. Ask your luncheon partner. He knows all about Otto von Preminger.

ZANUCK: Hey, keep me out of this.

HEDDA (*sighs*): Okay, Joe, sweetie, I'll go with your boring quote. You know where to find me. (*her voice starts to trail off*) Oh, by the way, Darryl, Marilyn Monroe has been dating Joe DiMaggio. Toodles!

Hedda leaves. Breen sighs heavily. Zanuck understands.

ZANUCK: I hear you.

BREEN: Pass the ketchup.

ZANUCK: I've got to tell you, Joe, you may have met your match in Preminger. He's a lawyer first, a director second, and difficult always.

BREEN: Even when you had him under contract?

ZANUCK: Especially when I had him under contract. But we were talking about *Niagara*.

BREEN: Lemme think about it and look at the Code again.

ZANUCK: Maybe we could add songs.

BREEN: Nothing closer than medium-long shot. And no side views.

ZANUCK: Otto Preminger came to me as an actor with stage background—a disciple of the grrrrrrrreat Max Reinhardt. He worked his way up, and by '44 was producing *Laura* with Dana Andrews, Gene Tierney, and Clifton Webb.

BREEN: I Remember. Necrophilia: a detective falls in love with a dead girl whose murder he's investigating. We ordered cuts.

ZANUCK: We made 'em, and the picture worked anyway. Otto wanted Clifton Webb. I didn't. Not because he's a fairy, but he's a dancer. But Otto took a camera crew and shot a screen test with Webb on his own against my direct orders.

BREEN: That's insubordination!

ZANUCK: "You son of a bitch," I told him. But the test was so good I signed Webb to a contract, fairy or not. *Laura* became a hit, and so did Otto. Eleven pictures later, he hits a slump, so—get this—he lets his contract run out. Goes to New York, stages *The Moon Is Blue*, and the S.O.B.'s back on top.

BREEN: What's he like as a person?

ZANUCK: A genius. An S.O.B. A genius S.O.B. Urbane, charming. Good producer. Did I say he was an S.O.B.? And a T.S.P.

BREEN: What's a T.S.P.?

ZANUCK: Tireless Self-Promoter.

BREEN: Likes the spotlight, eh?

ZANUCK: Like they say, he'd go to the opening of a letter. But he has the press on his side. Be careful, Joe. America doesn't like censorship.

BREEN: They like it when it's called self-regulation.

ZANUCK: Now about Marilyn Monroe.

BREEN: Not again.

ZANUCK: What about medium close-ups?

BREEN: Wet or dry?

ZANUCK: Umm—moist?

BREEN: Come on, Darryl.

ZANUCK: Medium close-ups dry, medium-long shots wet.

BREEN: Define medium-long shot.

Zanuck indicates by holding his hand at crotch level. Breen Shakes his head "no." Zanuck lowers his hand to his knees.

BREEN (cont'd): Deal.

The two men shake hands.

ZANUCK: Deal.

BREEN: But for God's sake not in 3-D!

ZANUCK: Is this a great country or what. Cigar?

Breen takes the cigar and the lights FADE, then come up.

ACT 1, SCENE 6—HEDDA HOPPER'S ALCOVE

This is an all-purpose area that serves as HEDDA's radio studio and newspaper office. It has a microphone, typewriter, and, of course, telephone. And she's on the radio wearing another hat.

SOUND: Beedley-beep-beep-beep news telegraph in b.g.

HEDDA: Hello from Hollywood, ladies and gentlemen. This is Hedda Hopper of the Chicago News Syndicate. Donna Reed, everybody's idea of a good girl, gets to play a bad girl in Columbia Pictures' *From Here to Eternity* which Fred Zinnemann is now shooting. I can't tell you the part she plays, but to get it past the Breen Office, they had to call her a "dance hall hostess." And speaking of censors, director Otto Preminger and playwright F. Hugh Herbert are about to start shooting their naughty stage hit, *The Moon Is Blue* on a closed set. Wonderful Bill Holden, charming David Niven, and newcomer Maggie McNamara are top-billed. And get this: Otto the Terrible says he refuses to make the cuts the Breen Office wants. He insists that movie audiences are mature enough to take it. Maybe so, maybe not. But are Preminger and Herbert able to take on Joe Breen? That's all the gossip from under my hat. This is Hedda Hopper in Hollywood.

Cross-fade to:

ACT 1, SCENE 7—PRODUCTION CODE OFFICES

Jack is making notes on a script and Emily is filing as Breen enters angry.

BREEN: Did you hear that? That noise?

Jack and Emily look dumbfounded.

BREEN (cont'd): That was a shot fired across our bow.

Breen reaches in front of Emily and whips a hanging file folder from the cabinet. He removes a script with a letter clipped to it, holds onto the letter, and slaps the script on top of the one Jack is reading.

EMILY: Who fired it?

BREEN: Who do you think? For nineteen years the Production Code has prevailed and I do not intend for Otto Preminger to be the first one to break it. He's already wined and dined Hedda Hopper. I want every call, letter, telegram and rumor about him or his picture that comes in or out of this office written down, typed, carbon-copied and filed.

He shows that the folder is empty.

BREEN (cont'd): This is gonna be full by the time we're finished. If anybody's gonna stumble on this one, it isn't gonna be us. Check?

JACK AND EMILY: Yes, Mr. Breen.

BREEN: And for God's sake don't let Martin Quigley think we're running scared, because we're not.

EMILY: I'm sorry, sir. Martin who?

JACK: Martin J. Quigley is the publisher of a trade paper called the *Motion Picture Herald*. He was one of the people who helped write the original Production Code in 1927.

BREEN: He's also behind the Legion of Decency.

EMILY: I thought the Catholic Church was behind the Legion of Decency.

JACK: They are, but by 1934 when Quigley felt we weren't enforcing the Code, he approached the Catholic Church and formed the Legion of Decency.

EMILY: This Martin Quigley sounds like quite an operator.

BREEN: The good news is the Production Code and the Legion of Decency put most local censorship boards out of business. The bad news is that people still see the Legion and us as the same thing.

EMILY: On a scale of one to ten, how bad do you think *The Moon Is Blue* is? I mean, really is?

BREEN: It's a ten. As far as I'm concerned, it's a ten pretending to be a zero. Most films, they are what they are: *These Three* was about lesbians; *The Story of Temple Drake* had violence and degenerate sex; *Convention City* had pretty much everything. But that was Hollywood, B.C.—before the Code. *The Moon Is Blue* is now. You'll see in the files that both Warners and Paramount slipped us the script last year sub rosa to see what we'd say, and we told 'em. Then Preminger-Herbert Productions sent it to us rosa and we sent 'em this.

Breen lifts a letter from the file and hands it to Emily.

EMILY (*reading*): Regarding *The Moon Is Blue* by F. Hugh Herbert, script dated December 11, 1952. (*reading*) "Donald Gresham is an architect. He meets a young girl, Patty O'Neill, in the Empire State Building. Donald invites Patty to his apartment for dinner intending to seduce her. He has just broken up with Cynthia Slater, who lives upstairs with her father, David Slater. David Slater is an amoral wolf who becomes drawn to Patty. Patty rejects both men's advances, insisting on keeping her virtue until she gets married—to Donald Gresham."

BREEN: There you have it!

EMILY: It sounds perfectly innocent.

BREEN: So it does. But you see, my dear, there are certain words here and certain ideas that are more than appear on the page. Later we wrote:

EMILY (*reading*): January 2, 1953. "Dear Mr. Preminger: We have read the script for your proposed production 'The Moon Is Blue' and regret to report that this material, in its present form, unapprovable under the requirements of the Production Code."

Breen gently takes the letter from her.

BREEN: Emily, you and Jack take the script and play the parts of Patty and Don. (*reading*) "We call your attention to pages 24 and 25 that contain unacceptable references to seduction."

JACK/DON: "We'll go to my place first and have a drink. How about it?" (*pause*) Emily, that's your line. (hearing no response). What's the matter?

EMILY: I'm trying to find my character.

JACK: Your character is Patty. She's the only girl on the page.

EMILY: No, I don't mean "character" character, I mean I'm trying to find my essence, my motivation.

BREEN: What do you think this is, an audition? Just read it.

JACK/DON: "We'll go to my place first and have a drink. How about it?"

EMILY/PATTY: "Would you try to seduce me?"

JACK/DON: "I don't know. Probably. Why?"

EMILY/PATTY: "A girl wants to know."

JACK/DON: "A girl is supposed to be intuitive about those things. I mean, you just don't go bluntly asking people such questions."

EMILY/PATTY: "I do. I always do."

JACK/DON: "And what if they say Yes, they're going to try to seduce you?"

EMILY/PATTY: "I usually believe them—and then I'm out one dinner."

BREEN: Stop right there. (*reading*) This unacceptably light attitude toward seduction places the material in violation of the Code." Now go to page 28 . . .

EMILY/PATTY: "Men are usually so bored with virgins. I'm so glad you're not."

BREEN: On page 36 there's another "virgin." Then Don says:

JACK/DON: Oh, yeah, that's me. (*reading*) "Why are you so preoccupied with sex?"

EMILY/PATTY: "Who, me?"

JACK/DON: "Yes, you."

EMILY/PATTY: "Do you really think that I am?"

JACK/DON: "Well, if you're always asking people if they're bored with virgins—or if they have a mistress—"

BREEN: Virgins, mistresses—now page 34, from "mistresses . . ."

JACK/DON: "If that isn't being preoccupied with sex, I don't know what is."

EMILY/PATTY: "But don't you think it's better for a girl to be preoccupied with sex than occupied?" (*laughs; then as herself*) Gee, that's kinda funny.

BREEN: No, it isn't. On page 58 there's the provocative statement, "He may have things in mind for after dinner."

EMILY: Excuse me, Mr. Breen, but don't people generally have something in mind for after dinner?

BREEN: Not in the movies.

EMILY: Dessert? Coffee? Apple tart—with an "E"?

BREEN: That's not what the script means. It means moola-boola.

EMILY: It doesn't say moola-boola.

BREEN: It may not say moola-boola, but it *means* moola-boola. The audience can tell moola from boola.

EMILY: Why do censors always want to protect other people but never themselves?

JACK: Search me.

EMILY: Could I?

JACK: That was just a figure of speech!

EMILY: But it sounds dirty, depending how you hear it.

BREEN: We represent the producers and the audience. We represent family values. We represent life the way it should be.

EMILY: Shouldn't movies represent life the way it is?

BREEN: Real life doesn't get a seal of approval. It's hard enough just getting a parking place. Whose side are you on?

JACK: Emily, enough.

BREEN: Film is a powerful teacher, Emily. They have to be made responsibly. People learn from movies.

EMILY: Yes, sir. You know what I learned? I learned that smoking is sexy. That you can sober up a drunk by filling him with black coffee. That Don Ameche invented the telephone. That when people are shot with guns, there's no blood, they just fall over. When a man forces himself on a woman, she pounds on his chest, but then gets so aroused that she kisses him back. And if'n you puts a knife under the bed it cuts the pain of childbirth in two. That's what the movies taught me. That's why I came all the way out here from Indiana —

BREEN (*interrupting*): "Pregnant."

EMILY: I wasn't pregnant! I came here because I wanted to.

BREEN: "Pregnant" is on page 57.

JACK: Do you know that when Lucille Ball got pregnant on *I Love Lucy* they wouldn't let her use the word? She was out to here but her own husband, Desi Arnaz, couldn't say she was pregnant. He had to say she was "spectin'." (*as Desi Arnaz*) "Go tell the Mersses that Lucy is 'spectin'. Babaloo." (*normal*) Ninety-two percent of Americans saw Lucy have her baby on January 20, 1953. I remember the date because the headline pushed the inauguration of President Eisenhower below the fold. Good thing Lucy wasn't really pregnant, only "spectin'."

BREEN: Are you finished? (*reading*) Page 102: the term "professional virgin."

EMILY: Who does that denigrate, amateur virgins? I'm just trying to get the hang of it.

JACK: It's like they took all the "Don'ts and Be Carefuls" and called it *The Moon Is Blue*.

BREEN: And those were just the highlights. I ended by telling them: (*reading*) "We regret to have to report unfavorably on this material, but under the circumstances it is the only opinion we can render in conformity with the requirements of the Production Code. Our final decision, of course, will be based upon your submission of a revised script. Cordially yours, Joseph I Breen."

EMILY: And then what happened?

BREEN: Nothing. I mean nothing. Preminger didn't even complain.

JACK: Do you think we're being set up for something?

BREEN: I'm sure of it, but that can't be my concern. The Code is the Code is the Code. Jack?

BREEN pulls JACK aside.

BREEN (*stage whisper*): This girl is a bit peculiar, but if we're gonna have to face Preminger, her questions'll keep us on our toes.

JACK (*stage whisper*): I hear you, Mr. Breen.

EMILY: So can I. It's a small office.

BREEN (*dropping stage whisper*): That's all for now. (to JACK) You hired her. The onus is on you.

Breen leaves.

EMILY: Am I in some kind of trouble?

JACK: I'm not sure.

EMILY: Whatever happens, I just want you to know that I would never, ever, no matter what Mr. Breen says, do anything to hurt you or your onus. (*pause*) And you have such a nice onus. (*pause*) Preminger's gonna cause trouble, isn't he?

JACK: If I was a producer and had my script rejected right down to the staples, I'd drop the project. Cut my losses. But Preminger's up to something. I just wish I knew what it was.

Cross-fade to:

ACT 1, SCENE 8: PREMINGER-HERBERT PRODUCTIONS OFFICE

Otto and Herbert pass a letter back and forth.

HERBERT (*reading*): "Our final decision, of course, will be based upon your submission of a revised script." (*normal voice*) That *was* the revised script! He's covering himself seven ways from sundown.

OTTO: I wish he wasn't such a good speller.

HERBERT: He's no fool, that's for sure.

OTTO: Just last week Breen okayed "From Here to Eternity," which has adultery, prostitution, knife fights, masochism, and disrespect for the military. We have two bachelors and one virgin. The Code makes America look simpleminded in a world where international cinema is setting a new standard for artistic expression.

HERBERT: These people are American, Otto. They're not European like us. We had salons, they had radio. We had Rembrandt, they have Norman Rockwell. We had the waltz, they had the Charleston. I can go on. They had Roosevelt—

OTTO (*interrupting*): — we had Hitler. And if that doesn't teach you the value of freedom, nothing will.

HERBERT: But Otto, it was only last year that the Supreme Court said the First Amendment even applied to movies. Besides, the Code isn't the law, it's a private agreement among the studios.

OTTO: A private agreement to deny artists and audiences their rights!

HERBERT: Stop practicing your quotes. The industry is bigger than you. Yes, even you. For heaven's sake, these the people who wanted to burn the negative for *Citizen Kane*—you think they care about *The Moon Is Blue*?

OTTO: This town is based on one rule: the rule of money. If they think it'll make money, it gets made.

HERBERT: What if it gets made and flops?

OTTO: Did the play not make money?

HERBERT: The play was a hit. In New York. New York isn't America.

OTTO: Who goes to the theatre in New York? Tourists. The same people will see the movie where they live.

HERBERT: America will line up to see Patty O'Neill *not* get laid?

OTTO: The Patty O'Neill you created is a nice virgin who does not want to go to bed with any man except her husband—when she gets one. All the Patty O'Neills will come to see the movie. And so will those women who remember when they were Patty O'Neill. And so will all the men who want to sleep with a Patty O'Neill. I think that takes care of just about every moviegoer in this country.

HERBERT: You're going to enjoy this fight.

OTTO: Fighting is publicity; publicity sells tickets.

HERBERT: No, for you, this is bigger than box office. You're on a crusade.

OTTO: I am not a crusader, but I know a holy war when I see one. Come on, Hugh, we have some heathens to crush.

Cross-fade to:

ACT 1, SCENE 9—PRODUCTION CODE OFFICES

Emily and Jack are alone.

EMILY: Where does Mr. Breen go at the end of the day? Not to the movies?

JACK: He goes home. He has a wife and six children.

EMILY: Six? Maybe he should go to the movies.

JACK: You've got quite a mouth.

EMILY: I'm glad you noticed.

JACK: It's what comes out of it. If I talked like you, Mr. Breen'd fire me quicker than you could say—*(can't find the words)*

EMILY: Say what?

JACK: Whatever it is, it's probably in *The Moon Is Blue.*

EMILY: Stop thinking like a censor. Let's get some dinner.

JACK: You're inviting me?

EMILY: Yes.

JACK: But you're the girl.

EMILY: Thanks for noticing. What do you say? *(when Jack makes no comment)* What's the matter? Code got your tongue?

JACK: I don't think we should see each other outside of work.

EMILY: Must everything here only go out over Mr. Breen's signature?

JACK: Gee, maybe I am taking this job too seriously.

EMILY: Tell you what. You buy groceries and I'll cook it at my place. Better?

JACK: Yes.

EMILY: Good, 'cuz it's the same invitation Don Gresham offers Patty O'Neil in *The Moon Is Blue*.

JACK: You tricked me!

EMILY: Oh, stop being a professional virgin. You'll be safe: I share a bungalow with two other girls.

JACK: Who just happen to be out tonight?

EMILY: No, they'll be there. Their names are Amber and Constantina.

JACK: What are they, exotic dancers?

EMILY: Almost. Actresses.

JACK: How'd you get mixed up with actresses?

EMILY: Because I'm—I'm one too.

JACK: Another coal comes back to Newcastle. Acting!

EMILY: Don't worry; it isn't catching. Six months ago I came out here from Indiana to be a star like Carole Lombard. But apparently she filled the quota, because every time I auditioned for anything it always seemed to go to somebody from Pasadena or to a friend of the producer. I didn't know producers had friends. So I put my Indianapolis High School home economics course to good use, opened the *Los Angeles Herald-Examiner* to "Help Wanted: Female," and I got cast in your show.

JACK: So you've stopped acting?

EMILY: No one ever stops acting. They just stop getting acting jobs.

JACK: That home economics course—how'd you do in cooking?

EMILY: Straight "A"s.

JACK: Your rewrite appears to satisfy the requirements of the Production Code. But we will, of course, base our final decision on the actual performance.

Jack and Emily head for the door.

BLACKOUT

ACT 1, SCENE 10—LEGION OF DECENCY OFFICES

MARTIN J. QUIGLEY stands uneasily before a seated MONSIGNOR PATRICK J. MASTERSON. Masterson is a little paunchy.

QUIGLEY: With all due respect, Monsignor Masterson, I ought to know how the Production Code works; I helped write it. Then when the studio heads ignored it, I sought solace in the church and, working and praying together, we begat the Legion of Decency that you now head.

MASTERSON: Stop reminding me of your credentials, Mr. Quigley. The problem is, as the publisher of the *Motion Picture Herald*, you're walking both sides of the street, and I'm never quite sure when you're at a crossing.

QUIGLEY: My heart and soul are with the Legion as they are with the church.

MASTERSON: But your wallet is with the studios. No matter how much you object to a film's content, your magazine never refuses a film company's advertising money for it.

QUIGLEY: I believe in freedom of the press.

MASTERSON: Your argument would be more convincing if you weren't a hypocrite.

QUIGLEY: I'm a good Catholic, Monsignor. But my paper has to appear neutral. The Legion of Decency and the Production Code may be cut from the same cloth but the garments are worn by two different entities.

MASTERSON: Why is this *Moon Is Blue* thing so important to you?

QUIGLEY: A growing number of filmmakers think the Code is old-fashioned, but I say morality never goes out of date.

MASTERSON: C'mon, Marty, what's your angle?

Quigley smiles at a fellow skeptic.

QUIGLEY: This is an opportunity to force the Production Code to take on the values of the Church.

MASTERSON: Keep talking.

QUIGLEY: Look: movies have been attacked in the past for profanity, violence, s-s-s sex p-p-perversion, ethnic slurs—clear-cut things that you know are wrong. But this Preminger picture looks so innocent that people won't know it's dangerous unless we tell 'em.

MASTERSON: Perhaps it really is innocent.

QUIGLEY: The more noise the Legion makes now, the more the Production Code will be put on the defensive. It's the same in politics: if we set the agenda, they have to fight on our terms. While they're in disarray, we step in.

MASTERSON: And what, run Hollywood? You visit the zoo, you don't live in it.

QUIGLEY: Hollywood is run by men who refuse to recognize the divinity of Jesus Christ.

MASTERSON: Martin, the heads of the film companies are already as Christian as they can get without being baptized. Louis B. Mayer is taking instruction from Bishop Sheen himself. Besides, churches should never mix in politics. We might lose our tax exemption.

QUIGLEY: But don't you see the beauty of it? The Legion can make the rules and the Production Code will draw the fire.

MASTERSON: The Production Code? Or Joseph Breen?

QUIGLEY: They're one and the same.

MASTERSON : The Production Code reflects society's standards. The Legion of Decency reflects the beliefs of the Catholic Church. If non-Catholics want to listen to us, so be it.

QUIGLEY: Why not be more ambitious?

MASTERSON: In America we have something called the separation of church and state. It's part of the same Amendment that protects freedom of speech. If the Church starts dictating speech, there would be a constitutional crisis.

QUIGLEY: Who do you think got Joe Breen his job? I leaned on Will Hays, and Breen knows if he veers even one degree off the straight and narrow, I can take it all back. Besides, I have a secret weapon. I tell you, *The Moon Is Blue* is a gauntlet tossed before us—a Rubicon of revisionism—a temple of temptation—a moat of morality—a portal to pornography—

MASTERSON (*interrupting*): Enough with the sermons, you don't have the collar for it. I read the play, and it seems pretty innocuous. It played for a year on Broadway and toured the country and nobody cared.

QUIGLEY: Yes, but deep within its blackened soul lies a festering pool of promiscuity and s-s-sexual in-your-end-o—

MASTERSON: I still don't understand how you'll know Joe Breen's plans.

QUIGLEY: I told you, it's a secret source.

MASTERSON: In that case, forget Church support. We don't have secrets, only dogmas.

QUIGLEY: Maybe if we call it confession.

MASTERSON: You can call it tuna fish for all I care. Tell me what you've got.

QUIGLEY: Since you insist—

Quigley crosses to the office door and opens it. There stands Emily.

QUIGLEY (cont'd): Come in, Miss Doakes.

Emily enters nervously. Masterson eyes both of them with suspicion.

INTERMISSION

ACT TWO

ACT 2, SCENE 1—HEDDA HOPPER'S ALCOVE

Herbert addresses the audience while, behind him, Hedda shuffles papers and straightens her hat, preparing to go on.

HERBERT: What with all the behind-the-scenes whoosis over *The Moon Is Blue*, it's easy to forget that we actually had to shoot the movie. Otto didn't forget. His direction of the actors showed his usual sensitive, gentle, delicate —

OTTO (*o.s.*) (*screaming*): No, no, no! You call yourselves actors? A trained dog could give better performances! Take it again from "Fade in"—and do it better!

HERBERT: The advantage of independence is that people leave you alone. And they did: we made the movie we wanted to make. Now all we had to do was persuade the Breen Office that it was cleaner than the script. And that meant going straight to the top.

Herbert exits to reveal Hedda.

SOUND: Beedley-beep-beep-beep news telegraph. Hedda is wearing another hat and reads from her script at the microphone.

HEDDA: Hello again, Ladies and Gentlemen, this is your Hollywood correspondent Hedda Hopper with the latest in movie news from under my hat. And what news it is! Producer Otto Preminger and writer F. Hugh Herbert—who are in open rebellion against the Breen Office's Production Code—are actually in peace talks with Joseph Breen himself. Breen has even consented to break bread in Otto's office. If you hear rumbling, it could be stomachs or it could be the clashing of personalities. At stake is whether Otto's half-million-dollar production will ever be seen by anybody except the censors.

ACT 2, SCENE 2—PREMINGER-HERBERT PRODUCTIONS OFFICE

Otto, Breen, and Herbert at lunch.

OTTO: I must say, Mr. Breen: Mr. Herbert and I never expected you to accept our luncheon invitation.

BREEN: You set a fine table, Mr. Preminger. You wouldn't have any ketchup?

OTTO: The press has cast us as adversaries, but that's unfair. We are all men of principle. I must commend you for having the courage of your convictions. So few in our industry do.

BREEN: This isn't courage, Mr. Preminger, it's pragmatism. If we don't censor ourselves, the government will.

HERBERT: With all due respect, you are fighting the wrong fight. The First Amendment to the Constitution prevents government censorship. Last year the Supreme Court even declared film to be an art form that deserves freedom of speech. This makes the Code superfluous.

BREEN: The Constitution doesn't have to face local censorship boards.

OTTO: Those are the enemy, not the movies.

BREEN: We can't go to court in every town that has a movie house. The Code effectively supersedes them.

OTTO: Did I tell you that we had two wonderfully successful sneak previews last week? At a theatre in Westwood—near the UCLA campus—it played like a charm. We also ran it in Pasadena. The white-shoe set applauded. We have over four hundred preview cards, all of them saying how much they enjoyed the picture.

HERBERT: Some of them even said they hoped the picture would not be ruined by censorship.

OTTO: Four hundred cards!

BREEN: That's not exactly true.

OTTO: Oh?

BREEN: We received one complaint. A father who'd taken his teenage son to see the main attraction when your film came on first. He said he was shocked for his son to hear "virgin" spoken on screen.

HERBERT: What was the main attraction?

BREEN: *High Noon.*

HERBERT: A western in which Gary Cooper has fistfights, kills three men dead, and his peace-loving Quaker wife shoots the fourth? And this man was offended by the word "virgin"?

BREEN: A complaint is a complaint. It shows you have a problem.

OTTO: We only have a problem when one person's taste is allowed to dictate what everybody else in a free society can see or hear.

BREEN: Stop being sanctimonious. You knew all along that *The Moon Is Blue* was unacceptable under the Code. What did you expect?

OTTO: I expect you to recognize what Mr. Herbert was saying: film is now protected by the First Amendment.

BREEN: We all followed that case closely. The Italian import *The Miracle* was banned in 1950 and boycotted by the church. Joe Burstyn, the distributor, took it all the way to the Supreme Court, which said that motion pictures are protected speech. Fine. Now *The Miracle* can be shown in theatres. But it doesn't get a Code seal.

OTTO: The film industry is not interested in the First Amendment?

BREEN: The film industry is not interested in offending anyone.

OTTO: Now *that* is offensive.

BREEN: You make censorship sound dirty. It's only good taste put in writing.

HERBERT: Which is precisely how we made our film. There's no nudity, no sex, no profanity, no killing, no destruction of property. I'm surprised it even got financed.

BREEN: Nevertheless, it cannot be released without cuts.

HERBERT: It would be like taking the Civil War out of *Gone with the Wind*.

BREEN: If you don't, nobody will ever see your film. Because without a Code Seal no theatre will show it. No family newspaper will advertise it. Priests will condemn it from pulpits.

HERBERT: These are the same churches that pray to a virgin?

BREEN: She's a different virgin!

OTTO: *The Moon Is Blue* has less sex than the Bible.

BREEN: It's the way your film makes fun of virtue.

OTTO: And in the end virtue wins. The virgin has the last laugh. Like in real life.

BREEN: Your picture makes fun of a virgin because she stays a virgin.

OTTO: It's a comedy! It has to make fun of something.

BREEN: Virginity isn't funny. Ask any man.

OTTO: Mr. Breen, you said that we can appeal our film to the entire Board. Let me ask you, has a ruling ever been reversed on appeal?

BREEN: No, but the hearing process has allowed producers to save face and compromise their films without compromising their integrity.

OTTO: In other words, stay professional virgins—Hollywood style.

BREEN: Listen, Preminger, you've been needling me the whole time I've been here. I've taken it because I've been stuck more times than a pincushion. But the bottom line is that the Code has done a goddamn good job for two decades, and it's not going to look the other way so a couple of hucksters sell a dirty movie. United Artists is a signatory to the Code, and they are obligated to uphold it. That's the only solution.

OTTO: On the contrary, Mr. Breen, you have suggested another one.

BREEN: And what would that be?

OTTO: It all depends on what the Appeals Board decides.

Breen folds his napkin and lays it on the table.

BREEN: You play your game, Preminger, and I'll play ours. You're fighting for one picture, I'm trying to protect the public from four hundred and ninety-nine others every year.

Breen storms from the office.

HERBERT: That's what I call throwing down a gauntlet.

OTTO: He's just angry over the ketchup.

HERBERT: He's right about the appeal. We're going to be making the same arguments to the same people who enforce their own Code. It's all a show. There's no way we can win.

OTTO: You make this sound like Clarence Darrow facing William Jennings Bryan at the Monkey Trial.

HERBERT: Clarence Darrow lost the Monkey Trial.

OTTO: But he got great publicity!

HERBERT: Publicity only works when people can buy your product, and if *The Moon Is Blue* is shut out of theatres, what do we do?

OTTO: We'll burn that bridge when we come to it.

ACT 2, SCENE 3—MARTIN J. QUIGLEY'S OFFICE

Quigley is on the phone.

QUIGLEY: This is Martin J. Quigley for Arthur Krim. Yes, I'll wait. (*pause*) Mr. Krim? Martin Quigley. I'm calling you because you're the top man at United Artists. I'll get right to the point. Otto Preminger is appealing *The Moon Is Blue* next week to the Production Code board. It's an important appeal and I'd like to offer my services. No, on your side. (*pause*) That's right, THE Martin Quigley. (*pause*) My services are beyond a fee. Besides, that's a matter for my advertising department. I shouldn't tell you this, but I was asked personally by Monsignor Masterson of the Legion of Decency to avoid a public showdown. No one can afford to lose face, Mr. Krim, certainly not United Artists. (*pause*) I'm only trying to help. Really! Hello? Hello? Mr. Krim? Hello?

Quigley has been cut off.

QUIGLEY (cont'd) (*to himself*): Okay, Krim, that was your chance; now we raise the stakes.

He taps the circuit button.

QUIGLEY: Sophie, get me Monsignor Masterson at the Legion of Decency. No, the private line. (*pause*) Hello, Monsignor, guess who just called me! Arthur Krim. He begged me to talk to the Production Code Appeals Board on his behalf. On his behalf! They're scared, is why! The more pressure the Legion puts on, the less wiggle room the Code has. Soon they'll be right where we want them. (*pause*) Of course I turned him down. The appeal is next week, and my secret weapon says that Joe Breen is preparing like a freshman facing his first college exam. He's worried if the appeal works, the Code starts to crumble. What do you mean, how do I know he's worried? I know. God bless you, too.

Quigley taps the circuit button again.

QUIGLEY: Sophie, send her in.

Emily enters, looking apprehensive.

QUIGLEY: Have a seat, my dear. Was it difficult getting out of the office?

EMILY: They let me go on auditions once in a while.

QUIGLEY: Don't become a movie star until we're finished.

EMILY: That was our deal, Mr. Quigley.

QUIGLEY: I never said I could make you a star, Emily, only that I could give you some nice publicity in my papers. We owe each other.

EMILY: Yes. I'm only in this position because I needed a job and you pulled strings for me. I feel like a spy.

QUIGLEY: You *are* a spy.

EMILY: It's not like I'm the Rosenbaums —

QUIGLEY: — Rosenbergs —

EMILY: But it still feels—I dunno—sleazy.

QUIGLEY: It is sleazy.

EMILY: And all this time I thought all I'd have to worry about was the casting couch.

QUIGLEY: Not everybody in Hollywood is like everybody in Hollywood. Now tell me what you've learned in Breenville.

EMILY: I don't think I should.

QUIGLEY: How would you like to be the only blacklisted it person in this town who isn't a Communist?

EMILY: Wow, you play rough.

QUIGLEY: Being clean is a dirty business.

EMILY (*pause*): Mr. Breen is preparing his case, but he's really waiting for you—I mean, the Legion of Decency—to make a move. He's had discussions with Mr. Johnston. They still oppose a Code seal for *The Moon Is Blue* but they want the Legion to draw the fire when it gets released anyway.

QUIGLEY: So United Artists intends to defy the Code too?

EMILY: And they're lining up United Artists Theatres to show it anyway.

QUIGLEY: Thank you, Emily. You can see yourself out.

Quigley gets up and leaves.

EMILY: But Mr. Quigley, wait! (*when alone*) You left before I could call you a creep.

ACT 2, SCENE 4—HEDDA HOPPER'S ALCOVE

Hedda Hopper—another hat already?—at her microphone.

HEDDA: Once again, Ladies and Gentlemen, this is your Hollywood reporter Hedda Hopper speaking from under my hat. Joseph Breen and Otto Preminger appear today before the Appeals Board of the Production Code Administration. This is the most important appeal in the Code's history; none other than Nick Schenck, the President of Loew's Incorporated, which owns MGM, will be in attendance. It's a closed session since they'll be discussing things that can't be discussed, at least not on the screen. A source from under my hat tells yours truly that even without the Code, the Legion of Decency is seeing red over the blue *Moon* and is set to launch a biblical crusade if the film gets a Code Seal. Starting right about now the best show in town is playing at the offices of the Production Code!

ACT 2, SCENE 5—PRODUCTION CODE OFFICES

Otto and Breen stand like debaters before Nicholas Schenck and the Board of the MPAA.

OTTO: Gentlemen of the Board; Mr. Schenck: the issue we face is not merely one motion picture. It is the artistic integrity of all motion pictures and the guarantee of the First Amendment to the United States Constitution. The Supreme Court has said that motion pictures deserve the right of free speech, and Hollywood must do the same. Mr. Breen?

BREEN: Gentlemen of the Board; my colleagues: the First Amendment indeed says that the government may not censor films. But it does not prevent our industry from censoring itself. We rely on the continued favor of the public and also their trust. If we abuse one, we shall lose the other. *The Moon Is Blue* is not the first film to run afoul of our Code of self-regulation. But it is the first whose producer has put his own welfare ahead of our industry's. Yes, Mr. Schenck?

Nicholas Schenck rises. He has a slight Russian accent and the passion to match.

SCHENCK: Mr. Breen; Mr. Preminger: Movies are family entertainment. I don't know why it's so hard for filmmakers to understand this. People go to the movies to get away from real life, not have it pushed in their face.

OTTO: But when they do choose to see something more serious, we should be able to provide it. Nobody is forcing anyone to see my film. With all due respect, Mr. Schenck, Mr. Breen has the wrong idea about *The Moon Is Blue*. It is a moral film. The girl gets the boy, the boy gets the girl, and the letch gets the boot. It's a love story with no other agenda.

BREEN: It is not a love story, it's a "free love" story. The Code clearly states that "free love" is not suitable subject matter, even if nothing happens.

OTTO: How can a film be immoral for taking a moral stand?

BREEN: The premise itself is immoral. You cannot discuss an immoral issue morally.

SCHENCK: Do you really believe that, Mr. Breen?

BREEN: It's an academic distinction, Mr. Schenck, but it's an important one.

SCHENCK: Is there a difference between a clean treatment of a dirty idea and a dirty treatment of a clean idea?

BREEN: I'm not sure the public is ready for that kind of—

SCHENCK: — because in the past we have made films about alcoholism, insanity, adultery, and even venereal disease and they've all gone out with Code Seals. What makes this film more dangerous?

BREEN: Those films all took their subjects seriously. *The Moon Is Blue* is a comedy and treats them lightly. In the other films, the transgressors were punished.

SCHENCK: In this film, the virgin stays a virgin. Isn't that punishment enough?

BREEN: Comedy says the virgin is screwy because she stays a virgin.

OTTO: Is Mr. Breen saying that if we take all the jokes out of a comedy, it gets a Code Seal?

BREEN: You could cut it down to the leader you thread the machine up with and it still wouldn't pass! There's going to be a public outcry against this film led by the Legion of Decency, and we'll be in the same spot we were in when I took over nineteen years ago.

As Otto recites a litany, Breen becomes increasingly agitated.

OTTO: I submit that the public has broken the code on the Code. They know when to roll their eyes when the see the hand of the Code. In just the last few years numerous pictures have violated the spirit of the Code and were awarded Seals because they obeyed the letter. Knife fights and adultery in *From Here to Eternity.* Cross-dressing in *Where's Charley?* Suicide in *Death of a Salesman.* Prostitution in *Miss Sadie Thompson.* Alcoholism in *Come Back, Little Sheba.* Even fairies —

BREEN: Fairies? Where?

OTTO: In *Peter Pan.*

BREEN: That was Tinkerbell! It's a Disney movie!

SCHENCK: Gentlemen, please! Control yourselves! Anyone who indulges in name-calling is a poo-poo.

BREEN: Mr. Preminger, I call your attention to an interview that your star, William Holden, gave last week in New York. Mr. Holden said that you, he, and writer F. Hugh Herbert agreed—before the picture even went into production—that the screenplay would not be submitted to my office for approval. He added, quote, "I didn't see anything unmoral about the picture," unquote. Here is evidence that you had never had any intention of following Code procedure.

OTTO: Gentlemen of the Board, like a soldier asked to follow illegal orders, I believe it is the right and the obligation of artists to oppose censorship and repression. We have not made a vulgar or obscene movie. We have simply raised questions that some people consider mature. That is what artists do, and that is why this country offers creative people so much opportunity. Do not take it away with a shortsighted decision. Thank you.

SCHENCK: Now, Mr. Preminger, you have made a very entertaining film. I know I speak for all of us when I say that we laughed and had a good time screening it. You are correct: there is no violence or profanity in the entire picture—just a few grown-up words that most people use every day. In this business at least.

OTTO: Thank you, Mr. Schenck. I'm glad you understand why the —

SCHENCK: However: we are not the American public. Yes, it's true that the girl is not seduced in the time she spends with the boy. But young people learn from what they see on the screen and use their imagination from what they don't see, and still other girls in a similar situation might get closer to the flame. Why teach them? I'm sorry, but I wouldn't let my eighteen-year-old daughter see your film.

OTTO: If she's eighteen, perhaps she should.

SCHENCK: I vote against a Code seal.

OTTO: I expected as much.

SCHENCK: You knew this when you made no changes in your script and filmed it anyway. The problem is now yours.

OTTO: I object, of course.

SCHENCK: Go ahead. It's a free country. This Board is in recess.

Schenck gavels the meeting closed.

ACT 2, SCENE 6—PREMINGER-HERBERT PRODUCTIONS OFFICE

Otto and Herbert sip coffee while Otto reads the trade paper.

OTTO (*reading*): Breen then added, according to this article, quote, the Board has reaffirmed its firm and wholehearted support of the Code. The Code has nothing to do with styles or changing customs. It is a document that deals with principles of morality and good taste. These are timeless.

HERBERT: Nick Schenck should win an Oscar for Best Performance by a mogul.

OTTO: At least the vote wasn't unanimous.

HERBERT: That's like saying, after they push you off the fortieth floor, "at least they didn't push me off the fiftieth floor."

OTTO: We still have one or two bullets in our gun. Don't take that television job just yet.

HERBERT: What television job? At this point I couldn't get hired to write a test pattern.

OTTO: Look at it this way, Hugh. At least you wrote the most morally objectionable work since *Lady Chatterley*.

HERBERT: Do you really want to know what inspired me? Right after I finished *Sitting Pretty* for Zanuck, a producer told me he had a love story he couldn't lick and asked me to help. He said, "My only problem is that the boy meets the girl in the first act and I can't think how to keep them from going to bed together right away." I explained to him that most women wait until they're married to have sex. The producer said, "Gee, I never thought of that." Well, from that it's only a hop, skip, and a virgin to *The Moon Is Blue*.

OTTO: Someday premarital and extramarital sex won't be so highly controversial.

HERBERT: Someday we'll not only be able to say sex on the screen, we'll be able to show it.

OTTO: I am not so sure that will be a good thing.

HERBERT: Why, Otto, I'm surprised to hear that coming from you.

OTTO: So am I! But the decision should be ours, not the censor's. I like to leave some things to the imagination. You don't watch a mystery if you already know whodunit.

HERBERT: If you knew why the Mona Lisa is smiling, would she be less beautiful?

OTTO: No, but she would be less interesting. Once you take the mystery and sex out of romance, what do you have?

HERBERT: Marriage.

The telephone RINGS. Otto answers.

OTTO (*into phone*): Yes, of course, put him through. (*to Herbert*) It's Arthur Krim of United Artists. (*into phone*) Good afternoon, Arthur. . . . Yes, he's right here. You're doing what? But it's never been done before! Of course I support you, I just never thought you would. What can I say? It's a brilliant move! I'm surprised I didn't think of it! Of course I'll tell him. Yes, of course. Good-bye, Arthur. God bless your thinking, and thank you.

Otto hangs up.

HERBERT: Come on. Out with it.

Otto dials the phone while Herbert stews.

HERBERT: Something's happened, and I want to know.

OTTO: You will. But I want to be able to give her the satisfaction telling her she's the first person I'm telling this to when I have the satisfaction of knowing she's not. (*into phone*) Hello, Hedda? This is Otto. (*miffed*) What do you mean, Otto who? I promised I'd tell you first.

Otto turns away from the audience, and Herbert faces them.

HERBERT: That's Otto: enjoying life to the fullest, even if it means death. But he was loving it!

ACT 2, SCENE 7—HEDDA HOPPER'S ALCOVE

Hedda perks up at the microphone and—oh, no, another farkakteh hat.

HEDDA: This is your Hollywood Correspondent Hedda Hopper with a big flash from under my hat. Flash! As I reported, the Appeals Board of the Production Code Administration has denied its official Seal of Approval to Otto Preminger's controversial sex comedy, *The Moon Is Blue*. Well, now comes word from one of my inside sources that United Artists, the film company that put up the money for *The Moon Is Blue*, has withdrawn from the Motion Picture Association of America and will release the film without a Code Seal! This has never before happened. The question now becomes whether any theatre will dare book this renegade film. And also what will the Legion of Decency do now that they stand alone in the fight? This is Hedda Hopper in Hollywood!

ACT 2, SCENE 8—OFFICE OF PATRICK J. MASTERSON

Quigley and Masterson, and the latter is not happy.

MASTERSON: Great work, Martin! "Let's make the Code take all the heat and we'll take over." Well, now they're martyrs and we're the ones roasting like Saint Lawrence. What were you thinking?

QUIGLEY: How was I to know that United Artists would resign from the Motion Picture Association so they could release the film?

MASTERSON: Your secret weapon is supposed to tell you secrets, not keep them.

QUIGLEY: Theatres still have to respect the Code. No Seal, no booking.

MASTERSON: You know theatre owners, Quigley. If they smell a hit, it's opening Wednesday.

QUIGLEY: The newspapers, then.

Masterson waves some newspapers.

MASTERSON: Preminger already screened the picture for the papers, and they're taking his side. (*reading*) Bosley Crowther, the *New York Times*: "As moral as a Sunday school book . . . virtue triumphs" and "Nothing that will stir forbidden impulses," the *New York Journal-American*. With notices like that, even I would see the picture! Oh, and then there's this one. Read it.

QUIGLEY (*reading*): "'The Moon Is Blue' is a delicious adaptation of the stage hit which will surely figure in any moviegoer's favorite list as the brightest and most originally charming light comedy of the year. It is hard to imagine a more irresistible piece." Hmph! Another fool.

MASTERSON: It's from *St. Joseph Magazine*, America's Catholic Family Monthly! It's our fool. They're using it for the quote ad.

QUIGLEY: We have to stay above the fray. Stay reverent. Dignified. How can we screw them?

MASTERSON: I don't see any other choice. We update the Great Boycott of 1933 into the Greater Boycott of 1953.

QUIGLEY: Yes!

MASTERSON: Enough of this minuet. If Hollywood will not or cannot police itself, the Church will provide guidance. But we'll do it from the pulpit, not the press.

QUIGLEY: Maybe we should pray for some kind of a sign.

MASTERSON: You pray for a sign. Me, I'm makin' some phone calls.

BLACKOUT

ACT 2, SCENE 9—PRODUCTION CODE OFFICE

Breen and Jack. Tearsheets all over.

BREEN: Suppose other film companies get the idea they can resign from the MPAA whenever it suits them and release a film without a Code seal. There goes our base.

JACK: They'll come crawling back after the film flops.

BREEN: Have you seen the reviews? They won't be crawling, they'll be dancing on our grave.

JACK: Maybe this is a signal, Mr. Breen. The landscape is changing. The breakup of the studio monopolies cleared the way for independents. A guy doesn't need a studio to be a producer any more—just a telephone, a business card, and a casting couch.

JACK: Mr. Breen, the Legion of Decency is positioning itself to step in where we can't go. Perhaps we should join forces.

BREEN: I'd rather French-kiss a light socket.

JACK: But the same people, Martin Quigley and Father Daniel Lord, wrote both our codes. We're already in bed together. Bad choice of words.

BREEN: The Code and the Legion have different mandates.

JACK: The public doesn't know the difference.

BREEN: Now you sound like Emily! Serves you right for hiring an actress. The difference is, the Legion publicly denounces pictures but the Code renders its decision and lets the industry police itself. Martin Quigley wanted us to draw the fire, but he's just made the Legion of Decency the bad guys.

JACK: I don't understand.

BREEN: You will by Monday morning. If I'm right, Sunday will be a day of rest for everybody except the sermon givers.

ACT 2, SCENE 10—HEDDA HOPPER'S ALCOVE

Hedda is back at the mike with—what is it by now, sixth hat? Seventh?

HEDDA: This is your Hollywood reporter Hedda Hopper with news from under my hat. Monsignor Patrick J. Masterson's Legion of Decency has spoken and the pulpits are sizzling over *The Moon Is Blue*. Cardinal McIntyre of Los Angeles announced in a letter read yesterday throughout the Archdiocese that, quote, "Viewing 'The Moon Is Blue' is hazardous and a violation of good moral conduct." The Archbishop of Philadelphia, John F. O'Hara, has issued a similar edict, and the Archdiocesan Council of San Francisco adds that the Code-less release of the film is "brazen" and calls it, quote, "a direct challenge to the public." And last but hardly least, His Eminence Francis Cardinal Spellman calls *The Moon Is Blue* quote "an occasion of sin for Catholics." He also urges Catholics everywhere to not only boycott this film but all motion picture theatres.

While Hedda holds forth, the lights come UP on Otto and Herbert in their office.

ACT 2, SCENE 11—PREMINGER-HERBERT PRODUCTIONS OFFICE

Otto and Herbert listen to Hedda's gabbler.

OTTO: An "occasion of sin?" I wonder if it's a formal occasion.

HEDDA: Flash! The National Council on Freedom From Censorship is weighing in. They are part of the American Civil Liberties Union. They say in their own statement that they support Otto Preminger's right to release his film, and they also support Cardinal Spellman's right to tell people not to see it.

HERBERT: Only the ACLU can come down on three sides of a two-sided issue.

HEDDA: The ACLU is going to have its work cut out for it, and so is the celebrated United Artists legal team. Police in New Jersey have arrested the manager of the theatre showing *The Moon Is Blue* on obscenity charges. The police stayed through the entire film, just to make sure. Massachusetts, Kansas, Ohio, and Maryland Censor Boards have gone even further and banned the film outright. Distributor United Artists has retained lawyers to fight the bans, and U.A. President Arthur Krim has stated that this is a showdown for the First Amendment. So it's Free Speech versus Free Love at a theatre near you, but maybe not for long. This is Hedda Hopper reporting from Hollywood.

ACT 2, SCENE 12—LEGION OF DECENCY OFFICE

No sooner does Hedda sign off than she stalks into Masterson's office. As she enters, Masterson and Quigley are already in conference as Emily waits obediently upstage.

HEDDA: Is the Pope on Preminger's payroll? Pardon my blasphemy.

MASTERSON: *Te absolvo*, Miss Hopper. Now that you're here, what's your question?

HEDDA: Are the Legion of Decency and Production Code in bed together or what?

MASTERSON: We're just friends.

HEDDA: Cut the hooey, Monsignor. Joe Breen may have lost control of that filthy picture but you haven't. Now then, and I ask this as a daughter of the church, what are you and Breen trying to pull?

MASTERSON: When people go to the movies, their minds are vulnerable. One seductive image on the screen can overrule the Sermon on the Mount.

HEDDA: Is this why the Legion and the Breen Office are merging?

QUIGLEY: Who said that?

HEDDA: Oh, don't play innocent, Martin! You've been playing both ends against the middle for years—ever since Joe Breen got the job and not you.

MASTERSON: Our two organizations are separate, Miss Hopper.

HEDDA: Then how come you're taking up their fight?

QUIGLEY: No comment.

HEDDA: There's a petition going around New York citing *The Moon Is Blue* as "immoral and unfit for showing." It has four thousand signatures so far.

MASTERSON: No comment.

HEDDA: Who got the Knights of Columbus picketing theatres? Who's giving the marching orders, the Holy Spirit? I may be a screaming harridan, but I'm a good reporter.

MASTERSON: No comment.

QUIGLEY: When two armies happen to be fighting the same enemy, does that mean they're under the same general?

HEDDA: If it walks like a duck and quacks like a duck and has feathers, it's a duck. I like ducks, but if yours lays an egg, it's breaking in my column. (*She finally SEES Emily.*) Who's the skirt?

MASTERSON: What skirt?

HEDDA: Lurking in the corner. I know a lurk when I see one. (*to Emily*) Step out of the shadows, dear. I'm Hedda Hopper. You can trust me.

QUIGLEY: She works for me.

HEDDA: I see. Or maybe I don't see. Maybe I'm not supposed to see.

EMILY: Oh, no, Miss Hopper, it isn't like that.

HEDDA: What's your name, honey?

QUIGLEY: Her name isn't important.

HEDDA: It will be if I put it in my column. Tell me, dear. Tell Hedda.

EMILY: I—I—?

Emily looks at Quigley and Masterson. Masterson nods his head.

EMILY: Emily Doakes.

HEDDA: You don't work for Quigley. You're with the Breen Office.

EMILY: No comment.

HEDDA: Nice talking to you.

Hedda leaves in as much a flurry as when she entered.

MASTERSON: What just happened?

QUIGLEY: Hurricane Hedda.

MASTERSON: Is she always like that?

QUIGLEY: Sometimes she's blunt. But she won't do anything to us. We're friends, to a point.

MASTERSON: So were Jesus and Judas—to a point.

QUIGLEY: Don't worry. She won't do anything to you because she's afraid of God. And she'll leave me along because I've got a newspaper.

EMILY: Where does that leave me?

QUIGLEY: I'll—why don't I—maybe she's —

MASTERSON: Wait outside, Martin. I want to speak with Miss Doakes alone.

Quigley looks at Masterson and sees he really means it.

QUIGLEY: I'll be calling you, Emily. At home.

Once Quigley leaves, Masterson warms.

MASTERSON: Do I make you nervous?

EMILY: No, Monsignor, but—I don't know.

MASTERSON: You were ill at ease even before that Hopper woman got here.

EMILY: I'm sorry, Monsignor.

MASTERSON: What I mean is—does Quigley have something on you?

EMILY: Pardon me?

MASTERSON: Why are you spying for him? There's no other word for it.

EMILY: I didn't plan to. I came to Hollywood to be an actress and couldn't get arrested. I interviewed with Mr. Quigley for a secretarial job, but it was filled. Then he said Mr. Breen was looking for a secretary and he'd put in the good word for me if I would—I guess that's spying, huh?

MASTERSON: Did Quigley ask anything else of you, my dear?

EMILY: No.

MASTERSON: Something more personal?

EMILY: No, Monsignor!

MASTERSON: Are you sure?

EMILY (*wising up*): You don't trust him either, do you?

MASTERSON: No comment.

EMILY: I told myself it's for a good cause. I've realized Mr. Breen and Mr. Quigley dislike each other, and I know I'm being used. I'm just not sure how. All of a sudden I feel like one of those words you can't say if you want a Code Seal.

MASTERSON: That's your conscience, Emily. Why don't you and your conscience go back to the office? I don't think you've done anything you need worry about. Just stop doing it.

Emily turns to leave but then turns back to Masterson and kisses his ring. He places his other hand on her head to bless her, and she goes.

As soon as she's gone, Masterson picks up his phone.

MASTERSON: Mrs. Coffey, would you get the Bishop on the line, please?

While he waits to be connected, Masterson grabs his chest. He groans and gasps and makes seizure sounds. He's having a heart attack. He drops the phone and collapses.

Moments later, Quigley reenters the office.

QUIGLEY: Hedda beat me into a cab, and then Emily ran past me— what did you say to her, Monsignor Masterson? Monsignor?

He finds the Monsignor on the floor and CALLS off.

QUIGLEY: Mrs. Coffey! Mrs. Coffey, call an ambulance!

ACT 2, SCENE 13—PRODUCTION CODE OFFICES

Jack works at his desk when Hedda and Breen emerge from Breen's office.

HEDDA: All I can say is if you're gonna die, die as a Monsignor. Cardinal Spellman throws a great funeral. Now I just need a quote from you about losing a worthy opponent, blah blah blah.

BREEN: There was much greatness in the man. He'll be missed.

HEDDA: You're a lousy liar, Joe. How do you think his death will affect the Legion of Decency?

BREEN: Masterson's assistant, Thomas Little. That's not the concern of the Production Code Administration.

HEDDA: Not Martin Quigley?

BREEN: Only when the Devil needs ice skates.

HEDDA: Was Masterson trying to put you out of business?

BREEN: The opposite. We both come from the same father. Daniel Lord and Quigley wrote the original Code and handed it to Will Hays. That kept the local censorship boards quiet for a little while, but when it was clear that it was being ignored, Father Lord and Monsignor Masterson created the Legion. Seeing the writing on the wall, Hays brought me in. That was in 1934.

HEDDA: And nineteen years later Quigley is pulling everybody's strings.

BREEN: You've been listening to Quigley.

HEDDA: If his collar went the other way he'd take over the Legion faster than you could say, "Nertz." I swear, that man can enter a room by oozing under the door.

BREEN: Remind me never to get on your bad side, Hedda.

Emily enters the office. She and Hedda see each other. Emily freezes. Hedda makes it clear that she notices her but acts as if she didn't.

EMILY: Mr. Breen? They're ready to screen the latest cut of *The French Line*. Oh, excuse me.

JACK: Emily, this is Hedda Hopper.

HEDDA: Hello, Emily. How long have you worked here?

EMILY: Only a few weeks, Miss Hopper.

HEDDA: I would swear I've met you somewhere else.

EMILY: I, I must have one of those faces.

HEDDA: Or two of them.

EMILY: Perhaps we—spoke on the phone—when you called Mr. Breen about—something.

HEDDA: I never forget faces, my dear. Only facts, figures, and quotes. (*laughs at her own joke*) *The French Line*, eh? I've been waiting for that. May I join you, Joe, sweetie?

BREEN: I'm afraid not, Hedda.

HEDDA: Oh, c'mon. I don't want to miss the first Jane Russell movie in 3-D. Howard Hughes says it'll knock BOTH your eyes out.

BREEN: Louella would kill me! Besides, it's a only a black-and-white work print with a temp score, a slop mix, and no opticals.

HEDDA: C'mon, Joe. For old time's sake.

BREEN: No, and that's my royal edict.

HEDDA: There's only one king in this town, sweetie, and that's Clark Gable.

BREEN: Haven't you heard? I'm the Czar. The Czar of all the rushes. Although sometimes I feel like King Lear raging against the storm. You understand.

HEDDA: A lot more than a sloppy printer with a one-time black-and-white score, or whatever you said. Where's your phone?

As Breen leaves —

BREEN: Use the one in my office. Jack, hold down the fort. Emily, see if Miss Hopper needs anything. So long, Hedda.

HEDDA: So long, Sweetie.

The moment Breen is gone, Hedda squares off against Emily as Jack watches.

EMILY: Miss Hopper, would you like some coffee?

HEDDA: No thanks.

Hedda goes into Breen's office and closes the door.

JACK: I'd swear she recognized you from somewhere.

EMILY: Nonsense. How would I know Hedda Hopper?

JACK: You may not know her, but she acted like she knows you.

EMILY: I guess I have one of those faces. All actors do.

Jack isn't buying it.

EMILY: Jack, have you ever done something that you wish you hadn't done, and you keep worrying about it, and it eats away at you, and finally you think you're gonna to go crazy, but then you find out that you really didn't do anything bad after all, so you start kicking yourself over why you were worrying about it, and then after a while it doesn't matter anymore?

JACK: Will this be on the test?

EMILY: It's just that I did something that I didn't know I was doing, but I kept doing it, and then when I stopped it turned out that it didn't matter even if I did do it, because it was already being done and it wasn't my fault.

Before he can answer, Hedda reenters.

HEDDA: Thanks for the use of the phone, Emily.

JACK: Any time, Miss Hopper.

HEDDA: You must be Jack.

JACK (*surprised*): Why yes!

HEDDA: Now excuse us.

*Hedda leads Emily back into Breen's office and
closes the door behind them.*

HEDDA: Listen, sweetie, cut the crap. I know you're feeding information to Quigley, and Quigley was passing it to Masterson. Well, Masterson's dead, so you're off the hook. And if you're smart, if Quigley leans on you, tell him to go pound sand. And if he says anything to me, I'll back you up.

EMILY: Why would you stick your neck out for me like this, Miss Hopper?

HEDDA: Us gals have to stick together.

EMILY: Gee, thanks, Miss Hopper. You're swell.

HEDDA: Stop playing the hayseed. You're smarter than that, so here's
how it works: I won't tell your boss—and I won't tell that nice
young man—if you do me one little, itsy-bitsy favor.

EMILY: I just want to do the right thing.

HEDDA: It is. You see, sweetie, you're more use to me here than you
would be collecting unemployment, which I can also arrange for, so
don't think about backing out. Am I going too fast for you?

EMILY: A little, around the curves.

HEDDA: I want you to be one of my inside sources.

EMILY: Is that ethical?

HEDDA: Of course not.

EMILY: I'll have to think it over.

Hedda hands Emily her card.

HEDDA: You do that, sweetie. Oh, and Emily, remember this: if you
can't find anything nice to say about someone—here's my private
number.

And Hedda leaves. Emily rejoins Jack.

JACK: What was that all about?

EMILY: Hedda Hopper wants me to be one of her spies.

JACK: Congratulations.

EMILY: You make it sound like an achievement.

JACK: No, but you held onto your job by telling me.

EMILY: I did?

JACK: Somebody in this building was leaking information. Now I know it wasn't you.

Emily laughs a little too hard.

JACK: What's that funny?

EMILY: If we play the cards right, the Production Code could have a direct line into Hedda Hopper's column.

JACK: I suppose we ought to run this past Mr. Breen.

EMILY: We will, but first I have to run something past someone else.

Jack is puzzled. Emily leaves.

ACT 2, SCENE 14—MARTIN QUIGLEY'S OFFICE

QUIGLEY: I didn't see you at Monsignor Masterson's funeral.

EMILY: I didn't think it was appropriate, Mr. Quigley. Judas didn't show up for the crucifixion.

QUIGLEY: You're no Judas. And Masterson was no Jesus. In ten years he won't even be remembered.

EMILY: Will the Legion die with him?

QUIGLEY: Not while there's a breath in my body. The new guy, Thomas Little, seems workable. I intend to bring about a complete merger of the Church and the Production Code. Together we can stop filth. You should be proud to be a part of it.

EMILY: You're barking up the wrong cross, Mr. Quigley. I'm no longer one of your apostles. I've seen how you work. You say you're fighting for a cause, but the only cause you believe in is Martin J. Quigley.

QUIGLEY: I see. All right, go away, Emily. I'm done with you.

EMILY: "Done" is right. You and your pathetic censorship are on the way out. They're lining up to see *The Moon Is Blue*. It's just good fluff, and the public agrees. It's only a matter of time before the Code is gone.

QUIGLEY: Not if I can help it, or your boss. You don't understand, Emily. Once the system is in place, it can be used to censor anything. Today it's movies. Someday it may be—anything else we say. The public must be protected.

EMILY: You side will lose.

QUIGLEY: Our side will win. Your side believes in respecting my side, whereas my side doesn't give a damn about you.

EMILY: This is America, Mr. Quigley. We'll just see who wins.

Emily leaves in a righteous huff. Quigley consults a small address book in his pocket and then dials.

QUIGLEY: Hello, this is Martin Quigley. May I have Cardinal Spellman, please? That's all right, just give His Eminence my best wishes and if he needs to discuss the new head of the Legion of Decency, he knows where to find me.

ACT 2, SCENE 15—STAGE APRON

Herbert enters and talks to the audience.

HERBERT: By the end of 1954, *The Moon Is Blue* had been cleared of all obscenity charges. It had also returned over four million dollars at a time when the average ticket cost forty-five cents. The German version—which Otto and I had the, ahem, foresight to shoot—did pretty well, too. As for Joseph Breen, that same year, the Board of Governors of the Academy of Motion Picture Arts and Sciences voted him a special Oscar—on his retirement. The awards were held on March 25, 1954, at the RKO Pantages Theatre in Hollywood.

ACT 2, SCENE 16—RKO PANTAGES
THEATRE HOLLYWOOD—BACKSTAGE

Otto and Breen find themselves waiting backstage.

OTTO: Well, hello, Mr. Breen.

BREEN: Hello, Mr. Preminger.

OTTO: Why not call me Otto? And I will call you Joe.

BREEN: You always could.

OTTO: Congratulations on getting the Award. You deserve it.

BREEN: If for no other reason thanks to you!

OTTO: I can't think of the Breen Office without Joe Breen.

BREEN: Geoffrey Shurlock is doing a good job. Maybe he'll give you a Code seal.

OTTO: *The Moon Is Blue* proves a picture can do well without it.

BREEN: Time will tell, Otto.

OTTO: The First Amendment did even better. But I will admit that, under the old Code, Hollywood made some damn good pictures— even if they couldn't say "damn."

BREEN: I always said that subtlety and wit beat vulgarity any day. Look at *Casablanca, The African Queen, Rebecca, Double Indemnity, Mr. Smith Goes to Washington*—

OTTO: You made them change all those pictures?

BREEN: And they turned out pretty well, don't you think?

OTTO: We'll never know how much better they could have been if—

BREEN: Now Otto!

OTTO: All right, Joe. That was then and this is now. As Zola said, "Truth is on the march and nothing can stop it."

BREEN: Zola never sold tickets until Paul Muni played him. People go to the movies to escape. Why show sex and killing and evil and profanity? We get enough of that in the streets.

OTTO: I am amazed that it takes a foreigner like me to explain to an American like you the value of freedom. The crime should be in not using that freedom.

BREEN: But can we handle all that freedom?

OTTO: Maybe Mr. Shurlock will let us find out.

BREEN: Perhaps he will. What's your next picture?

OTTO: The best-selling novel by Nelson Algren: *The Man with the Golden Arm*.

BREEN: Tell me it's about a man with a Midas touch.

OTTO: It's about heroin addiction.

BREEN: But Otto, drugs and drug trafficking are strictly prohibited by the Code!

OTTO: The message is so powerful that, after seeing it, even junkies will want to kick the habit.

BREEN: It doesn't matter. You cannot show drugs in any form! You'll never—

OTTO: Never what?

BREEN and OTTO together: Get a Code seal.

Both men laugh heartily. At last, they agree on something.

OTTO: I'll miss you, Joe.

BREEN: I guess I'll miss you, too, Otto.

ACT 2, SCENE 17—PREMINGER-HERBERT PRODUCTIONS—EPILOGUE

Herbert gathers his papers and packs his briefcase
while speaking to the Audience.

HERBERT: After collecting his honorary Oscar, Joseph Breen returned
to attending movies as a fan, not as a censor. He died in 1965.
Otto Preminger not only challenged censorship, he helped end
the Hollywood Blacklist by hiring blacklisted screenwriter Dalton
Trumbo to write *Exodus*, released in 1962. Otto died in 1986.

In 1961 *The Moon Is Blue* was quietly awarded a Code Seal—number
2-0-0-1-7—so it could be sold to television where anybody could see it.
The Legion of Decency is now known as the U.S. Conference of Catholic Bishops' Office for Film & Broadcasting. They still issue reviews and
long ago upgraded *The Moon Is Blue* to A-3: for adults only.

In 1968, Jack Valenti took over as head of the Motion Picture Association. One of his first acts was to replace the Production Code with a
Rating System. Valenti retired in 2004. That same year, the Federal
Communications Commission—which permits biased news, racism,
and anti-Semitism on radio and TV—fined Infinity Broadcasting
$500,000 because disc jockey Howard Stern made a bathroom joke. But
that's another story—or is it?

Hebert closes his brief case, turns out the lights, and exits.

CURTAIN

Afterword

Rereading the play after all these years, I was struck by how closely Arnie and I held to the facts, undoubtedly at the expense of drama. A comparison with the essay portion of this book will reveal the changes, combinations, and compromises that are, I was pleased to note, relatively nondestructive. True, we invented the platonic romance between Emily Doakes (a fictionalized character) and Jack Metzger (an obvious amalgam of the late Production Code Administration employees Jack Vizzard and Charley Metzger). But the broad strokes are there: Joe Breen's multiple rejections of *The Moon Is Blue*, Otto Preminger's ennui following his separation from Fox, Martin Quigley's hand in both the Code and the Legion of Decency, and Monsignor Patrick J. Masterson's death (October 9, 1953) a few months after the June 3, 1953, premiere of the film. In that regard, we were purposely vague about the calendar, but I don't think it significantly altered the time line.

Much of the posturing that is presented as public statements from Breen and Preminger is, in fact, taken from their actual press comments. As for their personal confrontations, those are, of course, dramatic speculation, as is the dialogue—but not the content—of Preminger's appeal to the Schenck board.

The Code was not evil, but it was facile, and it ultimately failed because it could not adapt to a changing society. This is something that Jack Valenti realized when he and his consultants devised the current rating system. It is also why the Valenti system has been under constant attack for its morphing standards. To his credit, Valenti admitted on numerous occasions that any legislation that cites the movie ratings (such as "no X-rated films") is patently unconstitutional because the letter designations are, by design, subjective and imprecise.

As Otto Preminger discovered, it's easy to tear something down. The real trick is what comes next.

Notes

Introduction and Acknowledgments

1. It didn't last. In *Miller v. California* (413 U.S. 15 [1973]), the Burger Supreme Court under President Richard Nixon reversed this and reestablished community standards as a guide for obscenity. To date, the Supreme Court has not revisited this regressive decision.

Chapter 1

1. ACLU, https://www.aclu.org/other/censorship-spotlight-film.

2. This is why there's rightly such a hue and cry when, for example, a president issues an edict that an agency such as the CDC or EPA hide studies or avoid certain language in published reports.

3. The ACLU has long opposed the Production Code for the reason that it is de facto censorship yet recognizes that it does not violate the letter of the First Amendment even as it violates its spirit.

4. There is a current school of thought that says the same thing about the advertising industry where an advertiser's false claims might be considered free speech rather than lies.

5. The list of scandals could fill a book, and, indeed, it did at least two: *The Hollywood Book of Scandals* by James Robert Parish (New

York: McGraw-Hill, 2004) and *Hollywood Babylon* by former child star and eternal scandal collector Kenneth Anger (New York: Straight Arrow Books, 1975). Anger's veracity can be challenged but not his vivid reporting.

6. British comedian/presenter Paul Merton made a highly credible attempt to untangle the case in "Paul Merton's Birth of Hollywood" (https://www.youtube.com/watch?v=dhTNkjTtQYU&t=61s).

7. That's a little over $1.7 million today.

8. Interview in 1983 courtesy of Gary H. Grossman. An estimated 50 million Americans went to the movies every week in the mid-1920s. Attendance jumped to between 90 million and 110 million in 1929, perhaps less because of the Production Code than the arrival of sound.

9. Hays's supremacy over what reached the screen earned him the sobriquet "Czar of all the rushes," referring to the daily footage shot by movie companies.

10. Quigley was an interesting character. He not only was a powerful trade paper publisher and stealth participant behind both the Code and, later, the Legion of Decency but also seems to have been an advocate for certain pictures in which he had a personal interest. It would be wrong to assert that he was on the take. It just sometimes looks like it.

11. MPAA Digital Archive, https://mppda.flinders.edu.au/history/mppda-history/1929-1932-creating-the-production-code.

12. Ibid.

13. Conversation with the author.

Chapter 2

1. One vital difference separated the two organizations, however: the Legion of Decency did not advocate government censorship, mindful of the constitutional separation of church and state.

2. Widely quoted, including at https://www.american-historama .org/1929-1945-depression-ww2-era/hays-code-facts.htm.

3. Gerald Gardner, *The Censorship Papers: Movie Censorship Letters from the Hays Office 1934–1948* (New York: Dodd, Mead & Company, 1987).

4. Hays remained an adviser to the MPAA for five years, during which time he dodged a historic bullet. When the House Un-American Activities Committee held hearings into Communist influence in movies in October 1947, it was industry spokesman Johnston who stood up for the Americanism of Hollywood and vowed that there would be no blacklist. A month later, in November 1947, he called a meeting of forty-eight industry leaders at New York's Waldorf-Astoria Hotel, where they created the blacklist.

5. Interview in 1983 courtesy Gary H. Grossman.

6. In 1986, the MPAA turned over five thousand files to the Academy of Motion Picture Arts and Sciences, which opened one thousand of the most noteworthy to researchers. Many of the citations in this book come from that trove.

7. *Casablanca* famously started shooting without an ending. Imagine Breen's reaction if Ilsa had left her husband to go off with Rick.

8. Jack Vizzard, *See No Evil: Life Inside a Hollywood Censor* (New York: Simon & Schuster, 1970).

9. Alas, neither the film's title nor the producer's name is identified.

Chapter 3

1. Wilder was being glib for effect. His family was murdered by Hitler.

2. Andrew Sarris, *The American Cinema: Directors and Directions, 1929–1968* (New York: E. P. Dutton, 1968).

3. The author won't identify it out of professional courtesy.

4. For a more complete discussion of *Laura* and the Code, see chapter 7.

5. *Hollywood on Trial* (1976), written by Arnie Reisman and directed by David W. Helpern Jr.

6. Ibid.

7. Preminger was so iconic as Mr. Freeze that, when the feature film *Batman and Robin* was made in 1997, the filmmakers hired another famous Austrian, Arnold Schwarzenegger, to keep with tradition.

8. For a more complete discussion of *Forever Amber* and the Code, see chapter 7.

9. As Lardner told the story, he and Preminger were working on the script when a call came in summoning Lardner to Zanuck's office. Preminger seemed hurt that the studio head had not wanted to see him, too. Only when Lardner returned to pack up his office did Preminger learn why.

Chapter 4

1. *United States v. Paramount Pictures, Inc.*, 334 U.S. 131 (1948).

2. This may be technically true, but in practice, if it had to be done, United Artists made the producer do it.

3. Titled *Die Jungfrau auf dem Dach* (*The Woman on the Roof*), the German cast featured Hardy Kruger (Gresham), Johannes Heesters

(Slater, called Slader), and Joanna Matz (Patty). These three actors also appeared as extras in the American version, and McNamara appears in the same capacity in the German version. In addition, David Niven starred in a West Coast mounting of the play. (Source: American Film Institute catalog)

4. Edward De Grazia and Roger K. Newman, *Banned Films: Movies, Censors, & the First Amendment* (New York: R. R. Bowker, 1982).

5. For more information on *St. Joan* and the Code, see chapter 7.

6. http://thepurplediaries.com/2016/09/29/moon-blue-motion -picture-production-code-otto-premingers-moon-blue.

7. American Film Institute online catalog.

8. By contrast, on November 29, 1953, the British Board of Film Censors classified the film as X, barring it to viewers under age sixteen. It could still be shown, however, in cinemas choosing to do so. On August 2, 1988, when it was released on home video in the United States, it was rerated PG.

9. Vizzard, *See No Evil.*

10. Separately referenced as *From Here to Eternity* (1953).

11. As noted in the text, the MPAA Board rejected Preminger's appeal.

Chapter 5

1. Broadway Theatre, December 2, 1943, to February 10, 1945; moving to City Center on May 2, 1945 (closing date unknown); and then reopening at City Center on April 7, 1946, to May 4, 1946. (Source: Internet Broadway Database)

2. *Hollywood Reporter*, July 9, 1952.

3. *Hollywood Reporter*, December 23, 1953.

4. Twentieth Century-Fox legal records quoted in the American Film Institute catalog.

5. American Film Institute catalog citing Twentieth Century-Fox records.

6. American Film Institute catalog (no citation given).

7. Based on the source novel by Prosper Mérimée.

8. Having replaced Colonel Jason Joy as Code liaison, McCarthy, a former brigadier general under George S. Patton, later produced the 1970 Oscar-winning film *Patton*.

9. Memo from McCarthy to Skouras, May 7, 1954 (AMPAS).

10. IMDbPro.

11. Jeff Huebner, "Full Nelson," *Chicago Reader*, November 19, 1998.

12. Trivers had written only one previous film, *The Men in Her Life* (1941). Trivers was not a front for Polonsky.

13. American Film Institute catalog.

14. Murray Schumach, *The Face on the Cutting Room Floor: The Story of Movie and Television Censorship* (New York: William Morrow and Company, 1964).

15. Internet Movie Database.

16. Jon Lewis, *Hollywood vs. Hardcore: How the Struggle over Censorship Saved the Modern Film Industry* (New York: New York University Press, 2000).

17. When Eric Johnston succeeded Will Hays as president of the MPPDA in 1946, he changed the name to MPAA, Motion Picture Association of America.

18. Lewis, *Hollywood vs. Hardcore*.

19. Ibid.

20. The film itself faced a more ignominious fate. In 2020, the same year it was voted for preservation by the National Film Registry, it slipped quietly out of copyright and into the public domain. At this writing, it is available on YouTube at https://www.youtube.com /watch?v=7_37-0ScCbw.

21. "The Top Box-Office Hits of 1956," *Weekly Variety*, January 2, 1957.

22. Gardner, *Hollywood vs. Hardcore*.

23. Lee Daniels, *Marvel: Five Fabulous Decades of the World's Greatest Comics* (New York: Abrams, 1991).

24. Roy Thomas, *Comic Book Artist 002*, May 1998.

Chapter 6

1. Joseph N. Welch was the attorney who took Senator Joseph Mc-Carthy over the coals as the televised 1954 Army-McCarthy Hearings were turning public favor against McCarthy. Welch achieved national fame and praise when he asked the senator, on live TV, "Have you no sense of decency, sir? At long last, have you left no sense of decency?" Although it was clever stunt casting on Preminger's part, Welch's performance, with a delivery that recalled his castigation of McCarthy, keeps the film from sinking under the weight of its serious subject matter.

2. Otto Preminger, *An Autobiography* (New York: Doubleday, 1977).

3. *Columbia Pictures v. City of Chicago*, 184 F. Supp. 817 (1959), 258–59.

4. "Wall St. Researchers' Cheery Tone." *Variety*. November 7, 1962.

5. Ibid.

6. Foster Hirsch, *The Man Who Would Be King* (New York: Knopf Doubleday, 1971).

7. Alan Schroeder, *Celebrity-in-Chief: How Show Business Took Over the White House* (Boulder, CO: Westview, 2004). Richard Nixon was offered a cameo role in the film but declined, correctly saying that a vice president newly ascended to president would not be permitted to cast the tie-breaking Senate vote.

8. Gore Vidal, *The Best Man* (New York: Signet, 1964).

Chapter 7

1. A curious observation given that neither Clifton Webb nor Vincent Price acted like linebackers for the New England Patriots.

2. Frank S. Nugent, "'Forever Amber' or 'Crime Doesn't Pay': In the Hollywood Version the Moral Lesson Will Be Underscored; Amber Will Suffer for Her Sins," *New York Times*, August 4, 1946.

3. *Newsweek*, October 16, 1944.

4. "Top Grossers of 1947," *Variety*, January 7, 1948.

5. Shaw shared his award, strangely enough, with Ian Dalrymple, Cecil Lewis, and W. P. Lipscomb.

6. When Preminger acquired the film rights to the novel, the price was erroneously reported as $795,000. This was the result of an editor pressing Preminger, "How much did you pay for the book?" and Preminger saying, "Seven ninety-five," meaning the $7.95 he laid out at the bookstore. The actual price was $100,000 (reported by Leonard Lyons, "The Lyons Den," syndicated column, November 25, 1964, and quoted on IMDb).

7. This was a clever comparison; *A Funny Thing Happened on the Way to the Forum* was a United Artists release that benefited Louis Nizer.

8. In contrast, the National Catholic Office for Motion Pictures gave the film a "C" (condemned) for its "superficial and patronizing in its treatment of racial attitudes and tensions" and for being "prurient and demeaning in its approach to sex."

9. "All-Time Film Rental Champs," *Variety*, January 7, 1976.

Chapter 8

1. Walter Wagner, *You Must Remember This* (New York: G. P. Putnam's Sons, 1965). Preminger's Paramount films were *In Harm's Way* (1965), *Hurry Sundown* (1967), *Skiddoo* (1968), *Tell Me That You Love Me, Junie Moon* (1970), and *Such Good Friends* (1971). Only *In Harm's Way* turned a profit. Its budget included digging a huge pit on the Paramount lot to fill with water to shoot sea battles with model battleships. When not in use, it was drained and used as a visitor parking lot.

2. Rossell, correspondence with the author.

3. Peter Bogdanovich, *Who the Devil Made It* (New York: Knopf, 1997).

4. Rossell, correspondence with the author,

Chapter 9

1. Based on seven major studios releasing one film per week plus short subjects, newsreels, and trailers, all of which had to be approved.

2. https://www.filmratings.com/Filmmakers.

3. This would later be changed to age seventeen.

4. Several early X-rated films were *Midnight Cowboy*, *The Devils*, *A Clockwork Orange*, *Birds in Peru*, *Fritz the Cat*, and the aforementioned *If*. . . . Not long afterward came the flood of sex films that self-applied the X for commercial rather than cautionary purposes.

5. Walter Reade of the Walter Reade Theatre circuit and owner of Continental Distribution.

Bibliography

American Film Institute catalog.

Anger, Kenneth. *Hollywood Babylon*, Bell ed. New York: Straight Arrow Books, 1975.

Balio, Tino. *United Artists: The Company That Changed the Film Industry*. Rev. ed. Madison: University of Wisconsin Press, 2009.

Bogdanovich, Peter. *Who the Devil Made It*. New York: Knopf, 1987.

Bouzereau, Laurent. *Cutting Room Floor: Movie Scenes Which Never Made It to the Screen*. New York: Citadel Press, 1994.

Cowan, Geoffrey. *See No Evil: The Backstage Battle over Sex and Violence in Television*. New York: Simon & Schuster, 1978.

Daniels, Lee. *Marvel: Five Fabulous Decades of the World's Greatest Comics*. New York: Abrams, 1991.

De Grazia, Edward, and Roger K. Newman. *Banned Films: Movies, Censors, & the First Amendment*. New York: R. R. Bowker, 1982.

Gardner, Gerald. *The Censorship Papers: Movie Censorship Letters from the Hays Office 1934–1968*. New York: Dodd, Mead & Company, 1987.

Haver, Ronald. *David O. Selznick's Hollywood*. New York: Alfred A. Knopf, 1980.

Hirsch, Foster. *The Man Who Would Be King*. New York: Knopf Doubleday, 1971.

Inglis, Ruth A. *Freedom of the Movies: A Report on Self-Regulation from the Commission on Freedom of the Press*. New York: Da Capo Press, 1974.

Kael, Pauline. *The Citizen Kane Book*. New York: Atlantic Monthly Press, 1971.

Leff, Leonard J., and Jerold L. Simons. *The Dame in the Kimono: Hollywood Censorship & The Production Code from the 1920s to the 1960s*. New York: Grove-Weidenfeld, 1990.

Lewis, Jon. *Hollywood v. Hard Core: How the Struggle over Censorship Saved the Modern Film Industry*. New York: New York University Press, 2000.

Malmuth, Neil M., and Edward Donnerstein, eds. *Pornography and Sexual Aggression*. New York: Academic Press, 1984.

McClelland, Doug. *The Unkindest Cuts: The Scissors and the Cinema*. New York: A. S. Barnes and Company, 1972)

Moley, Raymond. *The Hays Office*. New York: Bobbs-Merrill Company, 1945.

Parish, James Robert. *The Hollywood Book of Scandals*. New York: McGraw-Hill, 2004.

Phillips, Baxter. *Cut: The Unseen Cinema*. New York: Bounty Books, 1975.

Preminger, Otto. *An Autobiography*. New York: Doubleday, 1977.

Russo, Vito. *The Celluloid Closet: Homosexuality in the Movies*. New York: Harper & Row, 1981.

Sarris, Andrew. *The American Cinema: Directors and Directions, 1929–1968*. New York: E. P. Dutton, 1968.

Schroeder, Alan. *Celebrity-in-Chief: How Show Business Took Over the White House*. Boulder, CO: Westview, 2004.

Schumach, Murray. *The Face on the Cutting Room Floor: The Story of Movie and Television Censorship*. New York: William Morrow and Company, 1964.

Vidal, Gore. *The Best Man*. New York: Signet, 1964.

Vizzard, Jack. *See No Evil: Life Inside a Hollywood Censor*. New York: Simon & Schuster, 1970.

Wagner, Walter. *You Must Remember This*. New York: G. P. Putnam's Sons, 1965.

Credit Page Extension

Advise & Consent (Columbia Pictures, 1962). 1962. MS Hollywood, Censorship, and the Motion Picture Production Code, 1927–1968: History of Cinema, Series 1, Hollywood and Production Code Administration. Margaret Herrick Library. Archives Unbound, link. gale.com/apps/doc/SC5106218141/GDSC?u=gdscacc1&sid=bookmark -GDSC&xid=e854d2c6&pg=1.

Anatomy of a Murder (Columbia Pictures, 1959). 1959. MS Hollywood, Censorship, and the Motion Picture Production Code, 1927–1968: History of Cinema, Series 1, Hollywood and Production Code Administration. Margaret Herrick Library. Archives Unbound, link .gale.com/apps/doc/SC5106217406GDSC?u=gdscacc1&sid=bookmark -GDSC&xid=27fe8d51&pg=1.

The Production Code Administration "Analysis of Film Content" is reprinted with permission of the Motion Picture Association of America.

Carmen Jones (20th Century-Fox, 1954). 1954. MS Hollywood, Censorship, and the Motion Picture Production Code, 1927–1968: History of Cinema, Series 1, Hollywood and Production Code Administration. Margaret Herrick Library. Archives Unbound, link.

gale.com/apps/doc/SC5106215070/GDSC?u=gdscacc1&sid=bookmark
-GDSC&xid=7605107b&pg=1.

Forever Amber (20th Century-Fox, 1947). 1947. MS Hollywood,
Censorship, and the Motion Picture Production Code, 1927–1968:
History of Cinema, Series 1, Hollywood and Production Code
Administration. Margaret Herrick Library. Archives Unbound, link
.gale.com/apps/doc/SC5106203849/GDSC?u=gdscacc1&sid=bookmark
GDSC&xid=2465b570&pg=1.

Hurry Sundown (Paramount Pictures, 1967). 1967. MS Hollywood,
Censorship, and the Motion Picture Production Code, 1927–1968:
History of Cinema, Series 1, Hollywood and Production Code
Administration. Margaret Herrick Library. Archives Unbound, link.
gale.com/apps/doc/SC5106218969/GDSC?u=gdscacc1&sid=bookmark
-GDSC&xid=de5a6aa3&pg=1.

Laura (20th Century-Fox, 1944). 1944. MS Hollywood, Censor-
ship, and the Motion Picture Production Code, 1927–1968: History of
Cinema, Series 1, Hollywood and Production Code Administration.
Margaret Herrick Library. Archives Unbound, link.gale.com/apps/doc
/SC5106201646/GDSC?u=gdscacc1&sid=bookmark-GDSC&xid=9cc
6894b&pg=1.

The Man with the Golden Arm (United Artists, 1955). 1955. MS
Hollywood, Censorship, and the Motion Picture Production Code,
1927–1968: History of Cinema, Series 1, Hollywood and Production
Code Administration. Margaret Herrick Library. Archives Unbound,
link.gale.com/apps/doc/SC5106215685/GDSC?u=gdscacc1&sid=book
mark-GDSC&xid=81dbf372&pg=1.

The Moon Is Blue (United Artists, 1953). 1953. MS Hollywood,
Censorship, and the Motion Picture Production Code, 1927–1968:

History of Cinema, Series 1, Hollywood and Production Code
Administration. Margaret Herrick Library. Archives Unbound, link
.gale.com/apps/doc/SC5106214836/GDSC?u=gdscacc1&sid=bookmark
-GDSC&xid=e35491fa&pg=1.

Index

Note: photo insert images are indexed as *p1, p2, p3,* etc.

conflict, 90; *Carmen Jones* film and, x, 53–55; character and reputation, 31, 88–92; criticism of work of, 87–88; directorial beginnings, 32–33; directorial control and billing, 31–32, 87; education and law career, viii; *Exodus*, 33–34, 71, 72, 87; films from 1944 to 1953, 33; films from 1968 to 1979, 92; first Production Code encounter for, 77–78; *Forever Amber* film and, x, 36–37, 61, 79, 81; freedom of expression, 43, 92; Herbert partnership with, 40–41; *The Human Factor*, 90–91, 92; *Hurry Sundown*, x, 77, 84–85, 96, 240n6, 241n8; *Hurry Sundown* film censorship and, 84–85; last film flop and creditor suits, 91; *Laura* censorship fight and, x, 33, 78–79; legacy, 91–93, 103; *The Man with the Golden Arm* film and, x, 56–63; marriages and children, 91; *The Moon Is Blue* film and, viii, x, 37, 40–51,

92, 231; *The Moon Is Blue* film letter exchange between Breen and, 47–51; multi-picture deal with Paramount, 87, 241n1; as producer, x, 40–41, 71; *Saint Joan* censorship fight and, x, 43, 81, 83–84; *Skiddoo*, 92, 241n1; *Such Good Friends*, 92, 241n1; *Tell Me That You Love Me, Junie Moon*, 31, 34–35, 90, 92; treatment of actors, 31, 34–35, 88; at Twentieth Century-Fox, x, 32, 33, 36–37

Pretty Poison, 98

Production Code (Code): ACLU opposition to, 233n3; books on, vii; *Convention City* and beginnings of, 11–12; efforts made in scripts to adhere to, 18; enforcement of, 11; evolution, 103–4; failure of, 232; filmmakers cleverness in evading, 27–29; First Amendment and, 233n3; first film given seal of, p8; government censorship relation to purpose of, 103–4; MPAA impacts from, 60; 1927 appendices of, 10–11; on offen-